Cooperstown Conference On Professional Training

Needs, Issues, and Opportunities for the Future

CONFERENCE
PROCEEDINGS
November 16-19, 1989

Cooperstown Conference On Professional Training

Needs, Issues, and Opportunities for the Future

CONFERENCE
PROCEEDINGS
November 16-19, 1989

An AASLH Common Agenda Report
*Edited by Candace Tangorra Matelic
and Elizabeth Marie Brick*

COOPERSTOWN GRADUATE PROGRAM IN HISTORY MUSEUM STUDIES
*State University of New York, College at Oneonta
New York State Historical Association*

COMMON AGENDA FOR HISTORY MUSEUMS
American Association for State and Local History

COOPERSTOWN GRADUATE ASSOCIATION
Cooperstown Graduate Program in History Museum Studies

COMMITTEE FOR MUSEUM PROFESSIONAL TRAINING
American Association of Museums

The Cooperstown Conference on Professional Training was made possible by :

Cooperstown Graduate Program in History Museum Studies
      State University of New York, College at Oneonta
      New York State Historical Association

The Common Agenda for History Museums
      American Association for State and Local History

Cooperstown Graduate Association
      Cooperstown Graduate Program
        in History Museum Studies

Committee for Museum Professional Training
      American Association of Museums

Published by the American Association for State and Local History, an international non-profit membership organization. For membership information, please contact Director of Membership Services, (615) 255-2971.

Library of Congress Cataloging-in-Publication Data

Cooperstown Conference on Professional Training: Needs, Issues,
    and Opportunities for the Future (1989)
      Conference proceedings, November 16-19, 1989 / Cooperstown Conference on Professional Training: Needs, Issues, and Opportunities for the Future : edited by Candace Tangorra Matelic and Elizabeth Marie Brick ; Cooperstown Graduate Program in History Museum Studies . . . [et al.].
      p.   cm.
    Conference held Cooperstown, N.Y.
    ISBN 0-942063-08-2
      1. Historical museums—United States—Employees—Training of—Congresses. Museum techniques—Study and teaching—United States—Congresses. I. Matelic, Candace Tangorra. II. Brick, Elizabeth Marie. III. Cooperstown Graduate Program in History Museum Studies. IV. Title.
E172.C77   1990
907'.5—dc20
                                 90-1086
                                 CIP

Designed by Elizabeth M. Brick, Kenneth J. Chandler, and Candace T. Matelic. Typeset by Elizabeth M. Brick and Kenneth J. Chandler using an Apple Macintosh SE and Aldus PageMaker desktop publishing software in the Palatino font family. Provided to AASLH Press in disc form by the Cooperstown Graduate Program.

Contents

Preface: William T. Alderson

Of all the advances that museums and historical organizations have made over the last twenty-five or so years, it seems to me that none surpasses the increased professionalism of their staff members. Time was when very few of us had any training specifically focused on the jobs we performed. Indeed, most of us came into the field by accident. We trained to be historians, often with the assumption that we would become teachers in high schools or colleges. Then, in desperation for a job, we accepted employment in a museum or other historical organization, much to the scorn of our professors and academic friends who thought museum work was only suitable for graduate students who had flunked their prelims. There was virtually no place to go to obtain training for our "alternative career," so we learned by doing and by asking lots of questions at professional meetings.

That situation began to change in the 1950s and accelerated in the 1960s. The Williamsburg Seminar for Historical Administration, and the Winterthur and Hagley fellowship programs of the University of Delaware began in the 1950s. In 1964 the New York State Historical Association, under the leadership of Dr. Louis C. Jones, and with strong support from Board President Dr. Henry Allen Moe, began the Cooperstown Graduate Program in History Museum Studies. In the following year the National Endowment for the Humanities was created, and the same Henry Allen Moe became its acting chairman pending the arrival of appointee Barnaby Keeney. Seeking guidance on the development of NEH programs, Dr. Moe invited leading historians to meet with him in Washington. Lou Jones was one of the group, as was I as director of AASLH, and together we made an impassioned plea for training of museum professionals. This led directly to the NEH-funded seminar and workshop programs conducted by AASLH in the 1960s and 1970s, and these, in turn, led to some of the same kinds of programs run by the regional conferences of AAM, state museum associations, and many other groups.

The impact of NEH and National Museum Act funding on the growth of professionalism is not measurable but was enormous. Those of us who were involved in the training programs in the 1960s dealt with the most elementary subject matter, but with each passing year our participants became more knowledgeable. And as that happened museums themselves improved, educational requirements for jobs were raised, and markets for professionally trained people were created. Academic institutions lost their scorn for museum work and began programs of "public history" which offered museum and historical agency training and the prospect of employment in the end. The Williamsburg Seminar shifted from the recruitment of graduate students to the training of working professionals. The "ALI-ABA Course of Study, Legal Problems of Museum Administration" was held as a one-shot event in 1973 and has been an annual event ever since. And what was once called the Museum Studies Committee of AAM has just been admitted to standing professional committee status as the AAM Committee for Museum Professional Training.

From small beginnings a generation ago the professional training of museum workers has grown dramatically in numbers and importance. Beginnning staff members are already knowledgeable about the field, and more seasoned staff members have many opportunities to expand their knowledge and skills. The time has arrived to address new questions that have arisen over what the needs really are for our field, what issues need to be addressed, and what directions the training programs should take in the future. The many able people who attended the Conference on Professional Training last November have done an extraordinary job of identifying the needs, issues, and future directions, and the pros and cons of each. They have also issued a call to action that should be embraced by the entire profession. All of us, those who do the training and those who hire the trainees, have a stake in the outcome. We are, as a profession, where we are today because of the training programs of the past. We will be, in the future, the product of how we respond to the challenges the Conference has identified.

William T. Alderson, the retired President of Old Salem, Inc., was Director of the American Association for State and Local History from 1964 to 1978.

Cooperstown Conference On Professional Training

Needs, Issues, and Opportunities for the Future

CONFERENCE
PROCEEDINGS
November 16-19, 1989

Introduction: Candace T. Matelic

What were the goals of the conference?

    1) Strengthen the partnership between training programs and the field by bringing together a group of training providers and consumers to discuss needs, current issues, and opportunities for the future.

    2) Facilitate better communication among the providers of training programs (graduate and mid-career) through team analysis of existing offerings and discussion of professional standards for training.

    3) Increase awareness in the field by producing a "manifesto" covering issues such as the needs of different positions at different levels; balance of content scholarship and museology; role of institutions, individuals and training providers; impact of cultural diversity on training; and setting standards for professional training.Where did the idea for this conference come from?

How was the conference organized?

The format of the conference was modeled after the original Common Agenda conference (a group of 70 invited colleagues organized into "working groups"), with the important addition of an open, public conference for immediate response and feedback from the field.

Invited colleagues were organized into an Advisory Committee and nine Working Groups: three groups of training providers (representing national organizations, regional and state organizations, and structured programs, including academic programs and training institutions) and six groups of training consumers (representing administration, collections, education/interpretation, exhibits, research/scholarship, and small museums). The Advisory Committee included representatives of professional organizations and funding agencies.

Colleagues were consciously chosen to represent a mix of viewpoints, backgrounds, geography and professional interests, all within the constraints of space, and a shoe string budget that mandated co-sponsorship for the majority of travel and subsistence expenses. From the beginning, the conference coordinators were extremely sensitive to the inherent risks of structuring a conference to include an invited group of colleagues, particularly to potential criticism from those not included. But, it was very clear that this event was a step in a much larger process, rather than an end unto itself. We also knew that this was a reasonable way to produce the draft documents for peer review at the conference.

The Working Groups met all day on Friday, November 17, 1989. Advisory Committee members moved in and out of the groups throughout the day. A Cooperstown student served as recorder in each of the nine groups. Each group started with a set of questions. The Training Providers also worked with a draft copy of a survey of mid career training opportunities produced by the Smithsonian Institution's Office of Museum Programs. At the end of the day, a team of Cooperstown students took the draft documents and began entering them onto our computers. (They worked throughout the night and completed the draft documents by the reporting session on Saturday morning–an absolutely amazing feat about which conference participants still marvel!) While they were so hard at work, the public conference began Friday evening with a keynote address by Patrick Boylan, President of the United Kingdom Museum Association. Following the keynote, participants enjoyed a reception at the Cooperstown Program Headquarters which turned into a 25th Anniversary celebration towards the end of the evening.

Saturday morning, November 18, began with my overview address, outlining issues and trends that affect the current and future state of professional training. Then Mary Alexander facilitated the reports from the nine Working Groups. Following discussion and a break for lunch, conference participants reconvened in four groups to discuss current issues. These topics were:

— the balance of museology and subject content in training programs (long a controversial issue),

— the role of institutions vs. individuals (or who is responsible for training),

—real life, logistical concerns (ranging from money and time to access and child care—

whatever participants felt should be put on the table),

— the impact of cultural diversity on training (including recruitment, access, mentoring, internships, a clarification of terms and discussion of cultural sensitivity).

At the end of the afternoon, participants gathered once more for group reports and a summary of the conference by Dennis O'Toole. The evening was another Cooperstown milestone–a wonderful potluck supper for 150 people, cooked by Cooperstown students, based on recipes from a 25th Anniversary Cookbook (including entries from every class).

On Sunday morning, Cooperstown alumni met for their biannual business meeting while other participants visited the New York State Historical Association (Fenimore House and the Farmers' Museum) other area attractions (yes, there were a few baseball fans who enjoyed the Baseball Hall of Fame and Museum) or simply slept in. A group of Working Group and Advisory Committee members gathered for a post conference summary discussion during the afternoon. Although the original conference plans called for the group to articulate the next steps (an "action plan"), they instead had a general discussion, led by Mary Alexander, and defined a set of goals to guide future actions and activities. The afternoon ended with a verbal "Call to Action."

Where did the idea for the conference come from?

The idea for this conference evolved out of discussions with many colleagues in the field, in all the settings that one would expect to hear and have conversations about professional training: meetings of the AASLH Council (particularly the long range planning discussions), AAM's Committee on Museum Professional Training (formerly the Museum Studies Committee), alumni gatherings and conferences (most notably the Cooperstown alumni, but also the Seminar for Historical Administration), numerous conference sessions at annual meetings over the last few years (there have been plenty of these, always provocative, sometimes passionate), and numerous conversations among individual providers (Gail Anderson of the JFK Program, Bryant Tolles

of the University of Delaware, Frank McKelvey of Hagley, Dianna Thompson of Canadian Museums Association, Patricia Williams and Meg McCarthy of AAM, Carol Stapp of the GW Museum Education Program, Denny O'Toole and Bill Tramposch of the Seminar for Historical Administration–all come to mind immediately).

While the discussions built the foundations of the conference idea, the AASLH Common Agenda for History Museums, particularly its Interdisciplinary Task Force, provided the framework and support to develop it into an actual project. The Common Agenda began as a NEH funded collaborative project between AASLH and the National Museum of American History. At the initial conference in February, 1987, professional training was mentioned repeatedly as a concern by all four discussion groups . The Common Agenda quickly evolved into a movement of sharing, brainstorming, and collaborative projects. After the initial NEH planning grant period, the Common Agenda was endorsed by AASLH as a core program, and now functions as one of its regular departments.

Professional training was the subject of one of four "issue papers" drafted during the summer of 1988 and it appeared in final form, appropriately combined with the paper on scholarship, co-authored by Mary Alexander, Diane Jagodich and myself, in *History News* in May/June 1989. Mentioning Mary and Diane immediately brings to mind a few other key Common Agenda players: Doug Evelyn and Lonn Taylor of NMAH (who are responsible for the initial concept of Common Agenda) and Marsha Semmel at NEH (who has shared our long term vision of the potential of the Common Agenda particularly in the area of scholarship linkages). I must also mention Betty Sharpe at NMAH, who has regularly contributed to our thinking in her logical and crystallizing way, and has provided me with housing and food as well during the numerous meetings in Washington, DC. This brings me back to Mary Alexander. Mary contributed far beyond the normal call of her duties as Common Agenda co-ordinator, moving from a member of the planning team to co-ordinator of the conference. Her insight was particularly important as we struggled over the long list of names—all qualified and wonderful—

to develop the Working Groups and Advisor Members.

Two other forces contributed significantly to the conceptual shaping of this conference. A group of Cooperstown students, headed by Susan Kay Crawford, and including Elizabeth M. Brick, Eva Nagase, Stacey A. Otte, Mary Edna Sullivan, and Joanne Tupy, soon became known as the "conference committee." They started meeting in January 1989, and helped to mold the details of the idea, step by step, always asking how, who , where, when, and what if and why. It was important, all the way through, to have the direct input of these current "consumers." Their questions were relevant and immediate.

Cooperstown alumni, particularly board members of the Cooperstown Graduate Association, and the Cooperstown faculty also contributed to the thinking behind this conference. Motivated by the celebration of the Program's 25th Anniversary, both of these groups began discussing the needs and issues of professional training, particularly in the context of how the Program might serve the mid-career needs of its 600+ alumni in a more direct way in the next 25 years. Following an intensive self study in 1987 (which resulted in a revised and more comprehensive curriculum), we began discussing mid-career institute ideas and realized very quickly that we needed to know more from our colleagues in the field. We also realized that given both the breadth and depth of knowledge and skills alumni were requesting, and the increased number of possible training providers, we were really thinking about collaborative ventures among academic programs, professional associations and individual institutions. A conference seemed like a natural way to begin to get answers to our questions, and there was already precedent for such an approach since the Cooperstown Graduate Association had hosted an alumni conference on professional training in 1982.

It had been nearly a decade since the last Belmont conference when a small group of training providers hosted by the Smithsonian Institution's Office of Museum Programs met to discuss mid-career training in 1980. The universe had clearly changed, and the pace of rumblings about professional training had accelerated sig-

nificantly in recent years. The climate was receptive, the players were ready, and the timing was right. The Conference on Professional Training: Needs, Issues, and Opportunities for the Future seemed like an excellent way to garner momentum for the next decade of activity in professional training and human resources development. Although we knew the the issues would be relevant to the entire museum field, we consciously focused on history museums and historical agencies to keep the focus manageable.

How was the Conference funded?

The conference was a collaborative project. The funding came from the Cooperstown Graduate Program and its cosponsors, the State University of New York, College at Oneonta, and the New York State Historical Association; the Cooperstown Graduate Association; and registration income. The AASLH Common Agenda for History Museums supported Mary Alexander's time and expenses. Working Group and Advisory Committee members covered their own travel and some subsistence expenses, as did Patrick Boylan and conference participants.

A conference of this scale normally requires major grant support. This event happened, in large part, thanks to the hundreds of hours of volunteer time contributed by the Cooperstown students. They deserve credit and deep appreciation for this amazing effort.

Who is responsible for this Conference and Proceedings?

We all know that logistics, planning and organization make or break a conference experience for participants. If all goes smoothly, we remember the content of the meeting. If this does not happen, we remember what went wrong and have difficulty recalling the content. The arrangements for this event were handled masterfully by the team of thirty Cooperstown graduate students and the faculty and staff who assisted the effort.

Susan Crawford and the student conference committee, Elizabeth Brick, Eva Nagase, Stacey Otte, Mary Edna Sullivan, and Joanne Tupy, deserve special recognition for an effort far beyond the call of duty. Ken Chandler and Jessie Ravage led the crew of student recorders through the night-long frenzy to produce draft working reports. Betty Haas, Administrative Assistant for the Cooperstown Graduate Program, deserves a round of applause for handling the additional typing, copying, mailing, phone calls, supply orders, budgeting, and miscellaneous details during a year that was already overloaded because of numerous 25th Anniversary activities and initiatives. Mary Case, director of the Office of the Registrar, Smithsonian Institution, had the foresight to bring a lap top computer to the conference and shared a copy of her notes with the coordinators and a few discussion leaders to aid in the summary essays. As always, Mary Alexander was a delight to work with because she consistently followed through with hard work and enthusiasm. There were many other individuals who willingly pitched in during the conference, and shared their observations and appreciation afterwards. This recognition and support was invaluable during the long recovery period for the in house team—more than anyone realized.

Elizabeth Brick co-edited and co-ordinated the production of these *Proceedings* as a fourth semester independent study project, and patiently rearranged her own schedule as we waited for all of the contributing authors to send in their pieces. Ken Chandler designed the final copies of the nine Working Group reports. A group of students contributed to the Consumer Working Group reports following the conference. Their input was sent to the discussion leaders and integrated into the final reports. A team of colleagues including Mary Alexander, Pam Bennett, Doug Evelyn, Peter O'Connell, Denny O'Toole, Mike Smith, Susan Spater, Bryant Tolles, and Lanny Wright reviewed the draft in record time. We were grateful for their thoughtful

remarks and suggestions. We were also honored that Bill Alderson contributed his perspective to the preface.

There were so many colleagues who shared insights and encouragement throughout the planning and evaluation phases of this project. If we have inadvertently forgotten to mention anyone, please accept our humblest apologies.

Why was this conference important?

This was a seminal conference because it was the first time that so many training providers – representing national, regional, state and local organizations, academic programs, and history museums—met with their "consumers"— colleagues from a wide range of history museums and historical agencies, as well as current students from graduate programs to discuss professional training needs, issues and opportunities for the future.

Beyond the size and scope of this gathering, it was significant that the conference generated the written materials contained in these *Proceedings*. The Working Group reports and issue discussion summaries articulate a blueprint for action for the next decade and beyond, particularly in the area of curriculum. Training providers can look to this data, as well as the information on resources of providers, models of collaborative programs, and types of training programs that consumers think will address their needs, to guide their individual and collective program planning. If nothing else, the results of this conference reinforce the premise that professional training must be an active partnership of providers and the field they serve.

Candace T. Matelic is the Director of the Cooperstown Graduate Program in History Museum Studies.

PROLOGUE

Keynote Addess: Patrick J. Boylan
Issues and Trends that Affect Professional Training
   and Human Resources: Candace T. Matelic
Supplementary Documents

In the name of the International Council of Museums (ICOM), may I begin this happy event by congratulating the Cooperstown Graduate Program on two counts. The first is on achieving 25 years continuous provision of high quality and internationally respected postgraduate training for history curators, and second on the enterprise of Cooperstown, its sponsoring institutions (the New York State University College at Oneonta and the New York State Historical Association), the Cooperstown Alumni Association, and–not least–Candace Matelic, on organizing this timely and important conference. Perhaps the best evidence of my own faith in the quality of Cooperstown's training is that I employ a Cooperstown graduate as my Keeper of Leicestershire History, Jane Legget, who I understand is the only foreigner to ever run for office as Mayor of Cooperstown! It is also good for Pam and me to be here in this wonderful setting and to be able to use if only very briefly the splendid NYSHA facilities here. I am sure that without my time in the Library here I would never have discovered that I share my birthday with Davy Crockett, although he was born a few years before me.

Candace has asked me to set the scene for the weekend's discussion on these vitally important themes by first outlining the ICOM position, following my 12 years' service as an honorary officer of the ICOM International Committee for the Training of Personnel up to September 1989, and as a current member of the Executive Council of our world body (thanks in part to the support of my nomination by AAM-ICOM). Then I have been asked to update you on the very rapid but truly exciting changes currently in progress in the training field in the UK, and finally I will make some comments on the main conference theme – "Professional Training: Needs, Issues and Opportunities." Frankly, this is a very tall order for the 30 minutes allocated, but perhaps I dare speak rather more quickly that I usually do at international gatherings, in the hope that the current fashion for British accents in U.S. T.V. and advertisements will have made me more understandable than would have been the case a year or two ago.

First, the International Council of Museums, (ICOM) and professional training. Within a few months of its formation in 1947, ICOM, in partnership with UNESCO, saw the training of museum staff as an essential requirement for raising museum standards internationally. One of the earliest specialist International Committees to be established was one for the study of all issues relating to museum administration and personnel, including training, and in 1968, this was reformed by the 8th General Conference of ICOM as the International Committee for the Training of Personnel (ICTOP), with a specific initial mandate of producing, as quickly as possible, an International Common Basic Syllabus for Museum Studies training programs. Following detailed studies of existing syllabi and course structures and the publication in 1970 of a substantial review volume on the current state of museum training in the world, the Committee prepared the draft ICOM Syllabus as requested. This drew heavily on existing established successful practice, especially on the UK Museums Association's in-service Museums Diploma programme and the University training programmes in Brno, Czechoslovakia, and Leicester, England. The ICOM Syllabus was also considerably influenced by Georges-Henri Riviere, the pioneering French museologist and ICOM's first Director, and by Yvonne Oddon, of the ICOM Documentation Centre who together, following their respective retirements from full time office, became the ICOM Training Unit.

The ICOM Basic Syllabus was formally adopted by the 9th ICOM General Conference at Grenoble and Paris in 1971, and has subsequently been adopted–to a greater or lesser practical effect–by a substantial majority of the museum studies professional training programs of the world.

ICTOP has, since 1971, gone from strength to strength, meeting in 1972, 1974, and annually since 1976, and over the same period its active membership has risen from less than 20 to a current 220 full members, and a further 150 or so more non-voting members (i.e. ICOM members who have registered as voting members in another International Committee, but who want to participate in ICTOP in addition). We have had a substantial publications programme, including both conference proceedings volumes published regularly since 1978, a half yearly journal "IT" (Information on Training) since 1979, and review volumes, such as the recent UNESCO *Museum* special issue on training. Specific subjects reviewed, and which have been covered in detailed recommendations to ICOM, UNESCO, and the world museum profession, have included the requirements for university level professional training (1978), teaching methods and techniques in museum studies training (1979), basic museological training needs for personnel at all levels (including non-professional staff) (1981), mid career training (jointly with the Canadian Museums Association, 1982), museological principles and philosophy in museum training (jointly with the ICOM Museology Committee-ICOFOM, 1984), training for developing countries, especially the museums of Latin America (1986), the training of security personnel and the security training of professional staff (jointly with the ICOM Security Committee-ICMS, 1988), and conservation training needs of curators and the museological training needs of conservators (jointly with the ICOM Conservation Training Working Group, 1989).

ICTOP has a substantial research, meeting and publications programme planned for the coming ICOM Triennial Program through to the next General Conference In Quebec City 1992, including a joint meeting in the USA, and with the AAM Museum Studies Committee in August 1990, a joint meeting with ICCROM, the ICOM Conservation Committee and ICOMOS (the International Council on Monuments and Sites) in Ferrara, Italy, in May 1991, and a major programme of work to establish means and standards for assessment and evaluation of museum studies programmes. This last project is almost certainly going to be the most difficult, yet most important, task undertaken by ICTOP since the development of the Basic Syllabus 20 years ago, but we feel it is urgently needed. The explosive growth in the number of actual or purported museum studies training centres and programmes, without any information or guidance for either potential students or their future employers on standards is the most obvious evidence that the problem of quality as well as quantity must be tackled without delay.

I mentioned the 1970 review volume on museum training: that listed less than 50 museum studies training programmes world wide. By 1984, our joint Smithsonian/ICTOP directory–*Museum Studies International*, listed over 400, the 1988 edition more than 700, more than half of these in the USA. Yet the AAM Museum Studies Task force could identify less than 2 dozen of these that met simple quantitative (not qualitative assessment)–i.e. a minimum of 5 years of continuous operation and a minimum of 25 alumni. We have good grounds for suspecting that some of the museum studies "courses" that we currently list–not just in the USA but world wide–consist of nothing more than very brief timetable fill-ins for philosophy, anthropology, or art history faculty, with no personal museum experience, but who are short of an hour per week's teaching in their timetable, while other universities may be offering practical "training" internships for a half or full credit that amount to nothing more than unpaid College Museum stewarding or sales desk operations. We in ICTOP feel that neither ICOM nor, I am sure, the Smithsonian, should appear to be endorsing, by listing in an official directory, training programmes that are not worthy of the name, and where the students would probably be better off spending the time earning six and a half dollars per hour working in McDonald's in order to save up the money needed for a reputable and worthwhile professional training programme.

Finally, on behalf of ICOM, could I urge all non-members to check off the AAM-ICOM supplement when you next pay your AAM dues and become involved in the important work of our world body–once you are in AAM-ICOM, voting membership on the Training Committee, ICTOP, is free and your right. Similarly, on behalf of ICTOP, could I ask any AAM-ICOM members who are not registered with an International Committee to choose Training?

So far as the UK is concerned, we are currently in very exciting times. As I said earlier, 1989 has been not only the UK Museums Association's centenary year, and the 60th anniversary of the Royal Commission on Museums and Galleries that first proposed the establishment of professional training for museum work (something begun by the Association in 1930), but we have also seen the most substantial changes ever in the organization of museum training. At the end of December 1988, the 12 European community (Common Market) countries adopted unanimously a new international law that comes into effect on 1 January 1991, concerning higher professional qualifications and the mutual recognition of professional status–an essential requirement for the free movement of labour that is due to come into full effect at the end of 1992. The UK currently has no system of government recognition of qualifications and/or professional status in the museum field, and current Common Market plans to extend the new system of internationally recognized qualifications and professional status to cover intermediate and technical levels from 1992 gives added impetus to the need for urgent change.

Within the UK, the Museums Association had been pressing for direct government support for museum training for almost 60 years without success, but the new international climate and new national policies on the training of workers of all levels, has at last made progress possible.

Consequently, the Museums Association has been able to negotiate with the Minister for the Arts official government recognition and financial support, for the first time ever, for museum training. It is not possible, within the newly emerging government policies, for training funding to go directly to the Association itself, so a new organization, the Museums Training Institute, has been set up with direct government funding, through with the majority of its members being appointed by or though the Association. Out of a governing body of 16, roughly one third each come from the profession and from various categories of museum governing bodies, with the remaining third and an independent chairman (a leading businesswoman with national standing) coming from outside what the current government insists on calling the museum "industry." We have already recruited a first class Director, Simon Roodhouse, who has both museum and arts management training ex-

perience, and his three divisional heads are currently being recruited to take responsibility for—respectively—(1) training standards, (2) validation of qualifications and accreditation of both training centres and trainers (including e.g. the individual teaching faculty of training centres), and (3) marketing—especially the aggressive promotion of the need for training—together with research and development.

In my presidential address to our centenary conference in York in September, 1989, I called for a massive expansion in both financial and time commitment to staff training in all museums, large and small. In my view, a minimum of 2% of payroll costs must be allocated to staff training (a quarter of the current level of training support within successful large corporations). We also intend that by the time the new European community legislation comes into effect in 13 months time, at least the professional training standards for postgraduate professional training qualifications, full-time and part-time, will be established by the Museum Training Institute and the first two or three university programmes in this field will have been reviewed and given at least provisional validation and accreditation, so that the "class of '91" in each case will be assured of both a university master's degree (or other appropriate qualification) plus a Museum Training Institute endorsement that will carry an international standing.

Of course, the Institute will have many other tasks and levels of operation–not least in terms of updating training for existing museum personnel and the development of new training programmes and qualifications for the great majority of museum employees who are not curators–the only staff who have been catered for on any scale in existing UK museum training.

A detailed study, Training Needs and Skills Analysis, undertaken for the Association with the aid of Government grants over the past year showed that curators in the traditional sense now form only 14% of the UK museum work force–a 50% fall in 20 years in relative terms, and with probably an absolute net fall in total numbers in all areas other than local history museum curatorship, despite a near doubling in the total museum labour force over the same years, due in part to the creation of new jobs in non curatorial areas, but mainly to the creation of new museums, especially small social history museums.

As I said, in relation to both ICOM's training activities and current UK developments, the major challenge for the immediate future is, in my view, the establishment and assessment of standards for professional training. These standards need to be derived from a detailed assessment of skill and competency needs for different levels of museum work, set within an adequate coverage of the essential philosophy, ethical standards, and ideals of public service and education on which true museums are based. I am sure that graduate and postgraduate (in English terminology) training must not be reduced to a mere list of technical skills. If museum work is a profession, and I passionately believe that it is, then the philosophical and interdisciplinary basis of museums needs to be taught and understood as well.

Consequently, it has been firm and unambiguous policy within the UK Association for 60 years, and within ICOM for 20 years, that professional training must be based on a careful balance between an interdisciplinary understanding of the museum context in the widest sense, the professional application of the curator's (or future curator's) own academic discipline, museum management issues, together with properly supervised and structured hands on professional experience in museums with collections, resources and—not least—staffing relevant to the individual student's needs.

The next step for the UK Association—to be taken at our next Council meeting in two weeks time—will be the submission to the Museum Training Institute of the profession's views of the essential requirements for the validation and accreditation of graduate and postgraduate basic professional training programmes. The Association's Education Board was meeting yesterday to prepare the Association's draft submission. However, I am sure that this will include clear guidance on the interdisciplinary principle of the training curriculum, based on the ICOM Basic Syllabus, and on the practical content and work experience of the training programme. I am sure, too, that we will address the question of the qualifications of the teaching staff, with special emphasis on the need for them to have on appointment, recent, relevant and successful museum work experience, and to keep this up to date through practical working experience in real museum situations. We will also emphasize the need for active links with museums and working museum professional, and—not least—adequate physical and library resources to support the training programme. I hope that I will be able to send Candace a copy of the Association's final conclusions on these vital issues for publication in the proceeding of this conference, but would be glad to outline my own views on this in the course of the coming two days.

Patrick J. Boylan is the president of the UK Museums Association and a current member of the ICOM Executive Council.

Issues and Trends that Affect Professional Training and Human Resources: *Candace T. Matelic*

My purpose this morning is to provide an overview of some of the recent trends and activities, both inside and outside the museum field, that affect professional training. I hope that this summary will help us frame some of the significant human resource development issues and better understand the context for this conference.

We have definitely hit a sensitive chord. Given the current whirlwind of discussion and activity related to professional training, our discourse on this topic is timely and important. Many colleagues believe that articulating and implementing a strategy for human resource development is the major issue facing our field during the next decade and beyond. One could argue that this issue –taking care of people in museums–is more critical than collections, interpretation, preservation, ethics or professional standards, simply because all of these important concerns will be advanced only by the dedicated, talented, motivated, and trained people working in our field. Obviously, we all have a vested interest in this issue. Yet we know that it certainly is not an easy challenge.

We suffer from[1]:
   –limited financial resources for overall operations as well as training.
   –management styles that are still back in the late 1950's.
   –institutions claiming that training is a concern for individuals.
   –staff changing jobs on the average of every three years according to national statistics.
   –an exodus of staff in mid career because they cannot afford to stay.
   –burn out, low productivity, chaos, crisis management and stress.
   –jobs that increasingly require additional skills and knowledge.

Yet we know from numerous success stories in business and industry that:[2]
   –increased productivity is directly tied to the support and involvement of human resources.
   –people are happy, satisfied and motivated when they are helped to reach their fullest potential; specifically when they are given respect, responsibility, involvement in decision making and support for experimentation and creativity.
   –shared vision, power and information produces a quality product or service.
   –training is a key principle.

Many colleagues believe that articulating and implementing a strategy for human resource development is the major issue facing our field during the next decade and beyond. One could argue that this issue–taking care of people in museums–is more critical than collections, interpretation, preservation, ethics or professional standards, simply because all of these important concerns will be advanced only by the dedicated, talented, motivated, and trained people working in our field.

We may not agree on these ideas and philosophies, but regardless of our positions, let me suggest seven trends that affect our discussions about professional training.

1. The work force is changing significantly, which will affect who our "consumers" are and what real life concerns we must accommodate, both to employ and train them.

A sampling of the statistics we must pay attention to:[3]
   –Economists tell us that the labor force of the future will be smaller and that every skilled employee will be an increasingly valuable asset.
   –Demographers tell us that by 2020, 1 in 3 children will come from a minority group — African American, Asian American, Hispanic American, and others. Minority groups, combined with women, will make up the majority of new workers (15% of the current population is Hispanic; by 2020, 50% of the population will speak Spanish).

–Cultural diversity is the future. (White males will be a minority!)

—Women currently make up 50% of the work force; by 1992, 58%. Seventy two percent of working women have kids under 18, double the rate of 1955. In 1954, women waited 14 years after childbirth to return to work; in 1988, a woman was away 6-8 weeks.

—The concept of "family" is dramatically different. The traditional nuclear family with one parent working is less than 20%–and is a distinctly white middle class phenomenon that never applied widely to other groups.

—A "family" also means single parents and/or step families. One out of every four children born today is raised by a single parent. A third of all children born in the past decade will live in a step family by age 18. Half of marriages begun since the mid 1970's will end in divorce, and 60% of all second marriages will end the same way.

—Nine out of ten Americans have changed their lifestyles for health reasons in the last four years. Intoxication is now considered anti-social behavior, and 70% of Americans are now non-smokers. There have been major changes in our awareness of diet and nutrition and significant increases in the numbers of Americans who exercise regularly. The number one concern of convention planners now is the availability of health clubs or exercise facilities.

—There has been an increase in the average work week from 40 to 47.3 hours. One quarter of our work force works on Saturday; 15% works in the evening.

2. Our management culture is definitely changing toward a style focused on developing and using the full capacities of people.

Without getting into a history of the evolution of management theory and style,[4] we can summarize that during this century, we have moved from an authoritarian style, characterized by:
—formal lines of authority,
—standardization,
—explicit rules and regulations,
—centralized decision making, and
—division of labor.
Through phases where:
—the emphasis was on issues of motivation, communication, morale, feelings, self

esteem (using Maslow's hierarchy of needs, 1954).

—the focus was on employee participation, (the "quality circles"learned from the industrial quality control analyst, Dr. W.E. Demming); assuming that people like to work, can do so on their own, will accept and seek responsibility, can help solve a problem; utilizing the capabilities of people; and decentralizing decision-making.

Toward a human potential style/philosophy that:
—makes use of untapped resources (people)
—creates an environment which allows people to contribute to their full potential
— encourages full participation in important matters and self control, self actualization, and self direction.

We have begun to see these trends in history museums, through team design and development of exhibits and a variety of other "task forces," but we have yet to recognize this "risk taking" behavior in performance reviews. We can not assume that people know how to work in groups or teams; we must provide training in group dynamics and project management. Employee involvement is the trend of the future. In a wider range of issues, 90% of ideas for improvement come from the bottom up.

As John Naisbitt notes, human resources will give companies the competitive edge. (The United States is even better positioned than Japan in this area because of our diversity in culture which makes us more innovative. Compare Nobel prizes for example–U.S. with 154, Japan with 4.)

3. The nature of museum jobs is changing–in scope, technical complexity and degree of specialization, increasing demands on museum staffs and the need for training.

I mentioned new skills of working in teams and groups and the necessary knowledge of project management now affecting curators, educators, researchers, and designers, as well as administrators. The list of knowledge and skills goes on, and on, and on, ranging from people skills, to research, writing, and fundraising skills, to learning an ever expanding and changing world of technological tools (including computers, video, videodisk, holography, and fax machines. Fax has even become a new verb!). This trend is quite dramatic, if you compare job listings in *AVISO, History News Dispatch,* and other journals from 10 years ago and today. The statistics from two recent studies or surveys substantiate this trend:[5]

A **Canadian Labour Force Study** (February, 1989) which looked at job satisfaction in large and small institutions, income distribution, demographics, and occupational characteristics analyzed the supply and demand for labor and training noted that:

— the most frequently attended courses were in specialized or technical skills (administration and management courses rated highest for future consideration).

— employees viewed training as crucial to improvement of current job skills and future advancement. (Seventy-one percent of directors did not agree).

—those who left the field cited lack of institutional support for training as a major contributing factor.

An **AAM Museum Studies Committee Survey of Museum Studies Graduates** (1987-1988, 18 programs, 1200 graduates) found that:

— respondents viewed an MA degree as an important credential for entry into the field and advancement, but only one step in the process of career long learning.

—while only 24% returned to academia, (8% of the field, 15% prior to a museum studies degree acquired academic master's status), 74% attended professional training seminars and workshops and returned to attend other workshops immediately. (Over 33% attended workshops before attending a museum studies program).

4. All across the field, there is a call for the implementation and integration of current scholarship into our research, collections and interpretation.

Rare is the opportunity for a history museum staff member to stop and think, let alone research

and keep abreast of current scholarship.[6] Yet, there is strong consensus that this is critical to responsive and relevant collecting, research and interpretation. We know from the *Wages of History* survey (Charles Phillips, Patricia Hogan, AASLH, 1984) that the majority of people working in history museums or historical agencies have studied history at the undergraduate and graduate levels. Yet, very few have had a chance to upgrade their knowledge or keep abreast of current scholarship. A far fewer number have had any training in material culture.

This issue has been a core focus of the AASLH Common Agenda for History Museums and is certainly a "near and dear" subject for the National Endowment for the Humanities. Both are concerned with tightening the linkages between academic and museum scholars. We must commend the efforts of the Valentine Museum in Richmond, Virginia, The Chicago Historical Society, and the Atwater Kent Museum in Philadelphia for developing and financing programs with local universities to help their staffs improve their historical knowledge.[7] The Winterthur Museum deserves recognition for its ongoing material culture seminars, as does AASLH for the recent NEH supported "Past Lives, Past Places" seminar series.

Yet we must acknowledge that these efforts are rare in the field. There is much to be done in this area, from encouraging scholars in the academy to utilize museums and material culture in their work, to strengthening the support for research efforts of museum scholars. Museum scholarship should be evaluated regularly by the field, and excellence recognized in our awards programs and publications. We have the opportunity to build on the successful efforts of NEH over the past decade, but we must continue to explore ways to encourage and support long term collaborations and relationships between museums and the academy.

5. The universe of training providers has changed significantly, mandating cooperation, collaboration, and partnership to effectively serve the field.

There is no question that we have seen some dramatic shifts in who is providing professional training. There has been a movement from a few national organizations, academic programs and a handful of museums, to a great number of providers. Now some of the most active providers are regional and state organizations.

The increased number of providers and offerings certainly substantiates the widespread need for training. Yet, the situation is more complicated and confusing than ever. While we must commend and congratulate the Smithsonian's Office of Museum Programs for compiling both *Museum Studies International* (the most comprehensive listing of academic programs and internship opportunities at both undergraduate and graduate levels), [8] we must recognize the extreme (almost overwhelming) difficulty in sorting out the universe of options. It is important to note that it is not only students and beginning professionals who face an extensive task of researching programs to find the one(s) that satisfy their needs.

Colleagues who run our institutions face an equally (if not more) difficult situation as they attempt to hire qualified staff to fill their ever-changing vacancies. Many of us working in the field do not understand the qualitative differences between programs and offerings. If one scanned the mid-career offerings in any region for a given year, one would probably find workshops or seminars with the same or similar titles and yet very different curricula. The alumni of graduate programs and established mid-career institutes (such as the Seminar for Historical Administration or the Museum Management Institute) have difficulty staying up to date on the current curricula and focuses of the programs. The relative newness of many academic and mid-career offerings only compounds the problem.

The result is a continuing concern about the proliferation and uneven quality of programs and offerings. There is much more entry level or basic information than in depth or advanced information, and very little coordination of efforts as each provider attempts to cover the waterfront and reinvent the wheel. In some cases, there is more redundancy and competition between providers than is necessary or healthy. All of this raises many questions:
    —Is this situation a service or a disservice to the field?

    —How can we encourage providers to communicate, cooperate, and forge solid relationships to work together?
    —Partnership and collaboration are key words in our vocabulary, but what are the rules? What are the guidelines to successful ventures? Are there models we can look to (inside or outside the field)?
    —Beyond just professional organizations working together, how do we include individual institutions, consortiums of museums, and academic programs? All of these potential partners have resources to offer.
    —How will we coordinate efforts? We all know that facilitating a collaborative program or project takes much more time and communication, especially at the beginning.
    Fortunately, we have some good work to start from in exploring these questions.

6. We are in an era of ethics and standards, and there has been significant progress in defining guidelines and standards for training programs and individual offerings.

To begin with we must recognize the impact of the museum accreditation and museum assessment processes,[9] thanks to AAM, for reinforcing a climate of quality performance for museums. We should note that recently the accreditation materials pay much more attention to professional staff training.

To get a sense of perspective, it is useful to review the results of the two Belmont conferences,[10] sponsored by the Smithsonian's Office of Museum Programs and funded by the National Museum Act.
    —The conference in 1976 made recommendations that influenced standards for advanced degree programs, resulting in the establishment of an ad hoc Museum Studies Committee "to examine programs and establish standards."
    —The conference in 1980 focused on mid-career training. Participants noted the proliferation of programs, and expressed concern about quality and the lack of hard data covering needs and potential markets. They outlined goals and objectives for mid-career offerings and articulated guidelines (the group had trouble

with the word "standard"). It is interesting to note that they called for:

—an urgent consideration of the accreditation of programs.

—the AAM to serve as the home of a consortium of training providers who would be screened before admittance and pay dues.

—two publications: a directory of resources and offerings, and a guide to the selection of programs.

—the directors of national organizations to discuss data gathering, computerization, and a calendar of offerings.

It is interesting to note that OMP is committed to doing a *Survey of Training Opportunities for Museum Professionals*, and AASLH has produced a "History Calendar" which lists many training offerings. There has been continued discussion about accreditation, but there is not yet a program in place. There is not yet a consortium of providers, and now one decade after the second Belmont Conference, very little general knowledge or use of the guidelines for mid-career training.

The AAM Museum Studies Committee has evolved into the Committee On Museum Professional Training (COMPT),[11] a conscious move to broaden the scope of its activities to include mid-career offerings, the variety of training providers, and representation from the "consumers" in the field. In terms of standards, the committee has produced "Criteria for Examining Professional Museum Studies Programs" (published in *Museum News*, June, 1983), a comprehensive guide to evaluation of museum studies programs in 1985, and the "Survey of Museum Studies Graduates" in 1987.[12] Recent committee members have advocated the direction of accrediting graduate museum studies programs and have explored the issue through a task force appointed for this purpose in 1988–89. This group recommended a "recognition" program to the AAM Executive Committee and Council but it was sent back to the drawing board because it did not address all levels and forms of museum training.[13]

Responding to a wave of requests for information on training programs during the late 1970s, AASLH explored the concept of accrediting

training programs during 1980–84. A set of "Minimum Standards for Professional Historical Agency Training Programs" was developed by a small committee in 1980 and published in *History News*, July 1981. Although the orignal committee did not recommend a program of accreditation, the Standards, Ethics and Tenure Committee was charged with the task of implementing the standards. A program was piloted in 1982. Eighteen programs participated and after initial review, only three programs met the standards. The committee raised questions about the rigidity of the standards and recommended that the program be reexamined. Instead, they compiled the data from thirteen programs at eight schools and published a chart in the fall of 1984 in *History News*.

It is interesting to note that neither the AAM nor AASLH standards had an extensive field test (although one might consider the AASLH pilot a true consumer test)! Perhaps it is necessary to do more aggressive testing and refining of standards before the agenda of recognizing programs and offerings can be put into place and endorsed by the field. Certainly the AAM's museum accreditation program has benefitted by such process and scrutiny. We could learn from our Canadian neighbors' recent experience with personal certification. It may be useful to review the certification program of the Society of American Archivists[14] and keep tabs on the current activities in this arena of our British colleagues.[15]

In terms of curriculum standards, in addition to the American efforts of AAM, AASLH and many individual programs, we should note the progress of both ICOM and the Canadian Museums Association (CMA). In 1988, ICOM published the "ICOM Basic Syllabus for Professional Museum Training," developed by its Committee on the Training of Personnel (ICTOP). In 1978, CMA approved "Curriculum for Museum Studies Training Programs" (based on Lynn Teather's study of national and international museum studies curricula and responses to a survey of museum positions and training requirements in Canada in 1977).

The most current Canadian National Trainers Conference (Montréal, March, 1990) focused on a review of the CMA approved curricula and recommended revisions. The group also began to draft a "Human Resource Development Strategy" for the museum sector in Canada, building on their recent Labour Study.[16]

7. There has been a flurry of introspective or reflective activities including analyzing, revising and upgrading programs, and planning for the future.

Let me bring to your attention a plethora of recent Canadian activities:[17]
—There is government funding from the Department of Communication for training coordinators to meet and discuss common concerns and issues.
—In 1984, the focus was on "Issues and Answers."
—In 1987, the group addressed "Delivering Quality Training," (Proceedings have been produced for both gatherings).
—In 1989, the topic was "The Labour Force in Canada, Current Status and Emerging Needs."[18]

The ICOM Committee for the Training of Personnel (ICTOP) Conference,[19] (August 5-10, 1990, at the Smithsonian Institution, Washington, D.C.) focused on "Museum Training as Career–Long Learning in a Changing World," and "Career Development: A Shared Responsibility."

In recent years, there have been many self studies by individual programs and organizations. I'll just mention three as examples of these efforts:

Office of Museum Programs: [20]
—After 15 years, 1989 began an intense period of reassessment and redefinition. They adopted new objectives, including defining conceptual and ethical issues in museology for the field and training Smithsonian staff.
—They have reaffirmed the special emphasis on programs for Native Americans, Hispanic Americans, and non-western minorities.
—There has been a change from technical assistance and consulting programs to a graduated curriculum for entry, mid, and advanced professionals with accompanying instructional materials.
—They are currently evaluating all programs and have provided the Museum Reference Center with a larger and more accessible space.

Seminar for Historical Administration:
—After 31 years and 550 alumni, in April of 1989, there was an evaluation meeting of alumni, colleagues, other trainers, and sponsors. (It is a collaborative program of AAM, AASLH, Colonial Williamsburg, and the National Trust).
—They looked at audience and reaffirmed their commitment to mid-level training, potential leaders, and broader recruitment, including minorities.
–In terms of curriculum, they reaffirmed that they should provide the "cutting edge" in administrative expertise, actively involve participants in issues that cut across specific jobs or areas, and organized the curriculum into three areas: the historical administrator as executive, as cultural leader, and as career professional.
–They also developed a newsletter for alumni, changed from summer to fall, went from four to three weeks and sought a new source of funding for minority fellowships.

Cooperstown Graduate Program: [21]
—We undertook a year long intensive review of the curriculum. (The last review of this scope was in the late 1970's, and resulted in the change from a one-to a two-year program and the ending of the Folklife Program). The study involved all faculty, who began by developing a list of knowledge and skills that they felt museum professionals and our graduates ought to possess. The curriculum was then designed from this list.
—The study reaffirmed the Program's premises of training generalists, providing a solid foundation in all areas of museum work (while encouraging students to specialize in both a career track and an area of material culture), and balancing academic education and career training through a blend of theoretical information and practical skills and experience.
—The study resulted in a stronger museum studies core, team teaching for most courses, more field trips and special seminars, and accountability for practical skills on students' transcripts (now including computer skills, public speaking, writing, object analysis, planning and organization, and career planning, in addition to traditional collection, exhibition, photographic and publication skills).

—We also put more emphasis on teaching with objects and started a teaching materials collection.

Whew! In summary, while there has been a great deal of activity in the field in the last decade (with increasing pace in the last few years), there is obviously much work left to be done. The renewed interest in professional training is very encouraging and gives me hope that human resources development will be a major agenda item in history museums during the upcoming decade. I am quickly sobered when I realize that we are still at the point of raising awareness of many of these issues. All of this reaffirms the significance and timeliness of our gathering this weekend to discuss the needs and issues or professional training, and the opportunities for the future.

NOTES

[1] We do not have solid statistical data to support my assertions of burnout, stress or exodus of staff in mid-career. These statements are based on personal conversations and experience in history museums since 1970. For additional discussion about current training issues facing history museums see "Agenda for Our Future: The Challenge," *History News*, May/June 1989 by Candace Matelic, Mary Alexander, with Diane Jogodich.

[2] One only needs to scan the plethora of recently published management books to find support for this position. Thomas Peters' work instantly comes to mind. (*Search for Excellence*, with Robert H. Waterman, Jr. 1982, *A Passion for Excellence* with Nancy Austin, 1985 and *Thriving on Chaos*, 1987).

[3] Many of these statistics come from George Collins, currently the Director of Historical Interpretation at Colonial Williamsburg. George was for many years CW's Director of Human Resource Development and Director of Employee Relations and Communication, and has taught seminars in management of human resources for AASLH and numerous other organizations and institutions. He is a regular guest faculty member for the Cooperstown Graduate Program and I feel one of the most knowledgeable colleagues in the museum field about human resource management and development. Also see the Winter/Spring 1990 special edition of *Newsweek* devoted to "The 21st Century Family "for a quick introduction to the current meaning of "American family," and watch for John Naisbitt's new book *Millennium Trends–Megatrends of the 1990's*.

[4] Again I am indebted to George Collins, Colonial Williamsburg. My brief overview was based on George's seminar on Management Approaches and Skills, presented at Cooperstown in the fall of 1989, 1987, and 1985, and on a similar presentation at an AASLH Seminar in Management Techniques in 1983. I have just scratched the surface of this material and urge the reader to pursue this topic further. Those who are seriously interested in employee participation should know about the Association for Quality and Participation, 801-B, West Eighth Street, Suite 501, Cincinnati, Ohio 45203, (513) 381-1959.

[5] See "The Museum Labour Force in Canada: Current Status and Emerging Needs," February 1989, available from the Canadian Museums Association, 280 Metcalfe St., Suite 402, Ottawa, Ontario, CANADA K2P 1R7, and "AAM Survey of Museum Studies Graduates–Summary of Results," 1988 AAM Annual Meeting Sourcebook. See also the separate summaries in this section, "Summary of Museum Studies Training Issues in Canada," by Dianna Thompson, and "Committee on Museum Professional Training," by Bryant F. Tolles, Jr.

[6] It is important to note that scholarship means more than the traditional areas of history, art history, anthropology, science, etc. We must move beyond this narrow view and recognize that audience research, learning theory, educational psychology, organizational studies and management are legitimate and necessary fields of study for museum scholars.

[7] See "Staff Development: Innovative Techniques," Resource Report #8, Technical Information Service, AAM, for a description of the staff development programs at the Valentine Museum and the Chicago Historical Society. For more information about the program at the Atwater Kent Museum, contact John Alviti, Director. It may also be useful to look at programs of the Woodrow Wilson Foundation, "Teachers Training Teachers," a highly successful professional development program for high school mathematics and science teachers, and the "Academic Alliances in Chemistry" program; an idea that was adapted by the American Historical Association with workable formats that are easily adapted to mid-career and advanced training programs. The History Teaching Alliance program of the AHA and the Organization of American Historians in particular warrants our attention.

[8] *Museum Studies International*, 1988 edition is out of print. The Office of Museum Programs is soliciting ideas for content, format and distribution of a new edition. See the paragraph on OMP in the summary section of this *Proceedings* for more information regarding the Survey of Training Opportunities for Museum Professionals, currently underway.

[9] For more information about Museum Accreditation and Museum Assessment (MAP) programs,

contact the American Association of Museums, 1225 Eye Street, Northwest, Washington, D.C., 20005 (Patricia Williams for Accreditation, Kim Igoe for MAP). Also see "Accreditation: Self Study and On-Site Evaluation Questionnaire," Resource Report #4, AAM.

[10] See *Belmont Conference on Mid-Career Museum Training, Abstract of the Proceedings, May 9-11, 1980.* Office of Museum Programs, 1981.

[11] See the separate summary in this section on COMPT by Bryant F. Tolles, Jr. covering the history and current agenda of this AAM Committee.

[12] The criteria and evaluation documents are available from AAM as "Museum Studies Programs: Guide to Evaluation," Resource Report #3. The survey of graduates is cited in note #5.

[13] The AAM Special Task Force for Accrediting Museum Studies Programs was chaired by Vic Danilov. For more information, contact Vic or Bryant Tolles, the current Chair of COMPT.

[14] For more information, contact Donn C. Neal, Executive Director, Society of American Archivists, 600 South Federal, Suite 504, Chicago, IL, 60605 or (312)922-0140.

[15] See Patrick Boylan's keynote address in this *Proceedings*.

[16] For more information on Canadian activities, see the separate summary in this section of the *Proceedings* or contact Dianna Thompson at CMA, 280 Metcalfe, Suite 400, Ottawa, Ontario, Canada K2P 1RF or (613)233-5653.

[17] Ibid.

[18] See note #5.

[19] For more information, contact Jane Glaser, Special Assistant, OASM, or the Smithsonian Institution Office of Conference Services, ICTOP, S. Dillon Ripley Center, Suite 3123, Washington, D.C., 20560.

[20] See the separate summary in this section of the *Proceedings* or contact James Sims or Teresa LaMaster, Office of Museum Programs, Smithsonian Institution, Washington, D.C., 20560, or (202) 357-3101.

[21] See separate summary in this section of the *Proceedings* or contact Peggy McDonald Howells, Manager, Museums Studies, The Colonial Williamsburg Foundation, Drawer C, Williamsburg, VA 23187, or (804) 220-7211.

[22] Contact the author at the Cooperstown Graduate Program, PO Box 800, Lake Road, Cooperstown, NY 13326, or (607) 547-2586.

Supplementary Documents

Common Agenda and Training

In February 1987, at the Smithsonian conference that spawned "the common agenda," delegates raised the training of history museum personnel as a critical issue for the profession. The conference brought together seventy history museum leaders to identify common concerns and to create an agenda for action. The conference proceedings, published by the American Association for State and Local History, described the training agenda for museum personnel to be:

"The need for museums to collaborate with academic museum training programs and in-service programs to broaden their intellectual bases and achieve a better balance between vocational and scholarly content, particularly in the area of material culture."

In the fall of 1987, with funding from the National Endowment for the Humanities, two Common Agenda task forces guided the follow-up efforts under the auspices of the AASLH and the National Museum of American History. The Interdisciplinary Task Force kept the training issue as central to the Agenda's program planning. Specifically. the Common Agenda with the Smithsonian Institution's Office of Museum Programs and the American Association of

Museums offered a training workshop for workers in small to medium sized history museums in the summer of 1989. This workshop emphasized the need for museum workers to identify the intellectual mission of their museums and to insure that their collecting and programming reflected that mission.

Common Agenda is a national initiative that seeks to reflect common concerns and regards training as basic to this process. The focus on training is in concert with the traditional interests of AASLH and reflects the central role that the Common Agenda has assumed within the programs of the Association. As Common Agenda projects are considered, their potential for "training" the field is of prime importance.

In addition to providing training for and by the museum profession, the Common Agenda stresses collaboration in addressing the concerns of history museums and will encourage projects locally and at the state and national levels that bring trainers, employees, hiring institutions, and others with a stake in training for work with historical collections.

Mary Alexander

AAM Committee on Museum Professional Training

As museum studies programs developed nationwide during the fifties, sixties, and early seventies, the museum field became increasingly concerned with the need to establish standards for such programs–standards of a broad philosophical nature, as well as those specifically focusing on governance, administration, curriculum, faculty, students, financial support, facilities and resources, research, and placement. As an initial response to this perceived need, in 1973 the American Association of Museums created the Museum Studies Curriculum Committee which formulated a series of recommendations for the content of graduate and undergraduate courses of study. Soon following in 1976, came the Belmont Conference on Museum Training at which representatives of various museum related disciplines drafted a statement of basic principles relating to the purpose and substance of such training. Soon thereafter, Joseph Veach Noble, then president of AAM, appointed an ad hoc Museum Studies Committee, as *Museum News* stated, "to analyze and assess current museum training in relation to the professional needs of the museum community and the public it serves, and to recommend minimum standards for museum training programs." These basic standards, a statement on preparation for professional museum careers, and a list of museum positions with duties and responsibilities were published in a 1978 issue of *Museum News*, with a report treating suggested qualifications for museum positions, and hiring practices and salary and fringe benefit data appearing in the same publication two years later.

The committee's work productively evolved further when, in 1981, AAM's then president Craig Black requested that the Professional Practices Committee, through a subcommittee, examine the feasibility of accrediting museum studies programs. The outgrowth of this group's efforts was the important document, "Criteria for Examining Professional Museum Studies Programs," published in *Museum News* in 1983. The 1983-85 Museum Studies Committee next compiled a comprehensive guide to evaluation, to be employed by museum studies programs wishing guidance in carrying out a self study and up grading process. This document is currently available through AAM as Resource Report #3 of the Technical Information Service series. Feeling a need to learn more about what museum studies programs have or have not accomplished, in 1987-88, the committee, largely through the efforts of Candace Matelic and Gail Anderson, conducted a formal survey of the graduates of a selected number of such programs to collect some hard data about career patterns and professional contributions, and to draw some documented conclusions concerning the impact of the programs and their graduates on the museum field.

During 1987-88, the Museum Studies Committee continued to advance the idea of a formal accreditation or "quasi accreditation" (recognition) system for museum studies programs to be administered by AAM. In the summer of 1988, President Joel Bloom, following up on a recommendation made by his predecessor Robert MacDonald, appointed a special task force under the chairmanship of Victor Danilov to develop guidelines for the new system. The task force report, submitted in April 1989, was reviewed by the Executive Committee and Council of AAM and was accepted for implementation. The Museum Studies Committee was advised that whatever system is ultimately undertaken must be broad based to include all levels and forms of museum training, as well as being relatively simple and cost effective. In an effort to be more representative of the full spectrum of training opportunities available in the United States, the committee forwarded an application to AAM for permanent standing committee status under the name of the Committee on Museum Professional Training (COMPT), which was approved in May 1990. The committee is working on enlarging and diversifying its membership, creating subcommittees to study undergraduate, mid-career, and academic discipline-based training guidelines, conducting selective voluntary field testing of standards for graduate training programs, and continuing long range planning for the committee, the end product to be a written document giving purpose and focus to the business of the committee for the next one to three years.

Bryant F. Tolles, Jr.

Summary of Museum Studies Issues in Canada

Training co-ordinators from museum studies programs across Canada are funded by the Department of Communications, Government of Canada to meet for discussion of common concerns and issues in museum training. In 1984, the focus of the Trainers Workshop was on "Issues and Answers," in 1987, the meeting addressed the issue of "Delivering Quality Training," and in March 1990, the group will come together once again to explore the area of "Curriculum Development."

The Canadian Museums Association through its Professional Development and Standards Committee developed a curriculum for museum studies programs in 1976. This curriculum formed the basis for many museum studies programs that developed in Canada. By 1987, there were 96 different programs listed in the publication "Museum Studies Programs in Canada." They ranged from formal entry level programs at universities and community colleges, to certificates offered by provincial museum associations, museum management programs through continuing education and special seminars and courses.

It is time to examine the impact of the curriculum and revise it to ensure that museum studies programs can respond to the needs and demands of the future.

A recent study entitled "The Museum Labour Force in Canada: Current Status and Emerging Needs," examined the role of training in the museum labour force and recommended increased program evaluation to help the process of program renewal.

Currently, the Department of Communications of the Government of Canada is establishing a new Policy for Canadian Museums. Funding through the Training Assistance Program of the department provides financial support for training programs across Canada. The new policy will have an important impact on these programs.

The Canadian Museums Association provides financial assistance through its Bursary Program for individuals working in museums to attend training events both within and outside Canada. Mid-Career Development Grants are available through this program, and Fellowships are offered by the government through the Training Assistance Program.

In Canada, there are numerous training opportunities at the basic level, but due to the size and sparse population in some regions of the country, access to training is difficult.

The problem of access is even more severe at advanced training levels where opportunities are limited. The Museum and Art Gallery Management Program offered at the Banff Centre in Alberta and the Cultural Resources Management Program at the University of Victoria in British Columbia are the major continuing education opportunities offered at the senior management level.

There are only two masters level programs in museology in Canada. One is at the University of Toronto in Ontario and the other is a program offered in French jointly by the Université de Montréal and Université du Québec à Montréal.

The question of program equivalencies and standards for museum studies has been discussed by museum training co-ordinators, but not yet addressed.

Needs and issues seem to escalate, but there is always opportunity in Canada, especially with the strong financial support of government, to build on and strengthen the system of museum training.

Diana Thompson

Seminar for Historical Administration

Current issues will be the major focus of the 1990 Seminar for Historical Administration. Sponsored by the American Association of Museums, the American Association for State and Local History, The Colonial Williamsburg Foundation, and the National Trust for Historic Preservation, the annual seminar offers new historical organization administrators and those about to assume administrative responsibilities, the opportunity to receive in depth education and training. Applicants should also be full time, paid members of a staff for at least three years.

Changes in format, time of year, and length of program reflect the recommendations of a Spring 1989 conference of alumni, educators and museum administrators. Participants in the 1989 seminar and the resident coordinator, Gerald George, also suggested significant changes in curriculum and methods of presentation. Many of these ideas were considered and adopted by the representatives of the four sponsoring organizations. As a result, the 1990 Seminar for Historical Administration will be three weeks in length, from October 28 to November 17. Each of the three weeks will be devoted to one major theme. Presentations on issues relevant to each theme will be offered in full or half day sessions.

The first week will be devoted to the historical administrator as cultural leader. Leaders in the museum profession will present sessions on the issues of institutional mission, research, preservation of both sites and collections, interpretations, and evaluation. During the second week, the focus will be on the historical administrator as executive. Speakers will address issues of marketing, finance, personnel, legal questions, and politics. For on-site case studies, participants will travel to Montpelier, the home of James Madison, and to other nearby historic sites. This weekend of discussion and relaxation offers a unique opportunity to gain first hand information and to share experiences. The final week of the seminar concentrates on the historical administrator as career professional. Within this framework, each participant will have opportunities for self analysis, enhancing career skills, examining trends and challenges in the profession, and preparing to "re-enter" the work place.

Faculty chosen for the seminar will represent the "cutting edge "of scholarship and experience within the historical organization field. In most cases, issues will be presented by teams of two or three instructors, at least one of whom will stay over to deal with the following day's issues. This arrangement will provide a greater sense of continuity to the program and will also allow opportunities for participants to meet informally with faculty members.

Renewed interest in the seminar has been generated by the publication of two issues of the newsletter, *The Seminar Update*. Intended as a communication device, particularly among the over 500 alumni, *The Update* has received favorable comments from many of its readers. The editorial board plans to publish two issues each year.

Although sponsorship of the seminar and in-kind services are shared by all four historical organization agencies, the administrative responsibilities rests with the Office of Museum Studies of the Colonial Williamsburg Foundation. Williamsburg, Virginia is also the site of the annual seminar. Within the variety of professional development programs which are currently being offered, the Seminar for Historical Administration provides an opportunity for historical organization leaders to deal effectively with important issues facing their home organizations and in their professional careers.

Peggy McDonald Howells

WORKING GROUP REPORTS
TRAINING PROVIDERS

National Organizations
State and Regional Organizations
Structured Programs

Training Providers: National Organizations

Introduction

Our discussions, which began with a very basic review of what each of our organizations offered as training opportunities, revealed what became one of the critical concerns of the group as it finished its work. To wit, there are many training options available to museum professionals, but it is difficult to discover them and impossible to judge their value. This is a problem for the national organizations seeking to develop and offer appropriate training; and, more importantly, it confounds the potential learner as he or she tries to choose among training options.

Beyond the very practical concern of creating appropriate training opportunities and better disseminating information about them, the group addressed what we identified as the most important missing element of current training opportunities: the engendering of creativity, leadership, and a special quality that we termed "virtuosity." We struggled with how this neglected aspect of training might be addressed, wondering if models from industry and other professions existed. In the end, we determined that those models were not readily apparent to us. But, the need remains.

In addition to the need for encouraging creativity, the group also bemoaned the absence of training programs that attract a more diverse population of potential museum workers. The group discussed, with considerable frustration, the need to interest non-traditional museum employees in the field to allow us to better serve the needs of our audiences, real and potential. The participants agreed that models from other industries or professions should be sought out and adapted for our use.

A final concern addressed by the national providers acknowledged that training, whether pre-service or ongoing, is currently the responsibility of individual professionals. If this reality is to change, pressure must be put on institutions to position human development issues higher among the priorities of museums and their representative associations.

Mary Alexander
Discussion Leader

---

1. Using the OMP Survey and your working knowledge of the field, summarize the current offerings available for history museums in terms of content, audience and level.

OFFERING	OFFERING(continued)
General:	Self-study (individual, with institutional support and guidance)
Annual meetings	Career awareness and outreach programs
Pre-conference meetings	In-house courses
Conferences	Correspondence courses
Seminars	Certification programs
Workshops	Residency programs
Institutes	Reference/research
Symposia	Mentoring
Technical advice	
Publications/media	See Question #5 for some specifics
Criteria/standards established	
Self-study (institutional)	

2.   Assess the strength and weaknesses of this group of offerings. Note redundancies, gaps, and any other special characteristics.

STRENGTHS	WEAKNESSES	GAPS
Professional level workshops	Senior staff most often neglected	Small museums often neglected
Network, meet peers	High cost	How to determine and deal
Cooperative efforts	Exclusion of certain individuals and institutions through:	with transitions from entry to mid to senior levels
Educational efforts/programs responding to some perceived needs (i.e. weekend seminars)	Time constraints	Intellectual aspects separated from technique at present
Range of choices	Money commitment	Sabbaticals
Opportunities to step back and reassess	Limited pool of applicants and number accepted into programs	Commitment to professional training by institutions not a given
Sense of accomplishment, reward, enrichment	May leave participants with false sense of expertise	Neglect of those on the "fringe of the system," not in the mainstream:
Best offerings exploit talent, are focused, give results	Lack of directed/focused training	Emerging organizations
	Poor identification of entry-level and management issues	Volunteer-run
		Not associated with national organizations
	Difficulty in defining level (where does entry level end?)	Culturally diverse organizations
	Difficulty in finding good instructors	Need to understand changing demographics
	Difficulty in defining good leadership	Filling in where community support fails
	Difficulty in defining and assessing needs	Financial support
	Talent/virtuosity not fully exploited	
	Little structured mentoring	
	Not enough *or* too much focus (need balanced curriculum)	
	Lack of shared information about offerings	
	Assumption that everyone will professionalize	
	Assumption of a certain level of expertise at outset	

3. What attributes and resources does your group of providers bring to potential collaborative training programs?

NPS—system of training: entry level and performance improvement; managerial and financial support for employees to gain out-of-house training

SAA—programming structure, curriculum; workshops, conferences, seminars; bringing workshops to regional areas; certification program based on education, expertise, and on an examination

AASLH—access to small museums around the country; consultation/technical assistance programs; intensive training seminars; Common Agenda for History Museums

AAM—wide range of museums; national policy influence(?) and access; annual meetings, seminars; task force on museum education to identify training gaps and needs

OMP, Smithsonian—established, ongoing program with tiered curriculum; residency program (internships, visiting professionals); career counseling; training of faculty to work with curriculum

National Trust—liaison and resource from preservation to history; different point of view (lots of non-professional members)

4. Are there any restrictions/limitations regarding potential collaboration/partnership efforts that should be noted?

Different agendas/focuses

Limited cultural diversity of collaborators, shared assumptions, exclusivity (out-of-bounds for some?)

Prepared to follow-through and follow-up? - ongoing commitment and mentoring

Limited success in dealing with volunteer groups

Funding restrictions: need to make money

Training is an institutional commitment, not to be taken as a given

Need for a central data base, communications, being informed

Need for planning meetings away from national meetings

Need for internationally-minded commitment

5. Has your group of providers been a partner in collaborative training programs? Are there specific successful programs inside or outside the field that we should highlight as models?

American Law Institute, American Bar Association (ALI/ABA):
    Learning from experts within and outside of museum field
    Deals with current issues
    Oriented to senior level
    Ongoing planning group
    Scope of program very focused in structure and content
    Produces authoritative literature
    Immediate feedback

Modern Archives Institute:
    Entry level
    Quality instruction
Mellon Fellowships to the Bentley Library:
    Senior level
Winedale Seminar:
    Brings people together at various stages of careers
    Intensive
    Result-oriented

A.A.S.L.H. Interpretation Seminars:
    Current
    Quality instruction
    Intensive
    Result-oriented
	Museum Management Institute
	N.A.M.E. Workshops
	Fulbright Fellowships
	American Society for Training and Development
	Major Corporations - I.B.M., Xerox...

6.   Burning Issues.

Role that training plays in rejuvenation of staff Improving the sharing of information about training Intellectual content needs to be incorporated into skills training Tension between institutional *vs.* individual	needs Training is a political issue; needs to be recognized and dealt with as such Training as a continuum, ongoing developmental process Need to acknowledge and develop strategies for dealing with cultural diversity and changing demographics

The members of the Training Providers: National Organizations working group were—

Mary Alexander, Program Coordinator, Common Agenda for History Museums, American Association for State and Local History (Discussion Leader)

Meg McCarthy, Director, Meetings and Continuing Education, American Association of Museums

James Sims, Acting Director, Office of Museum Programs, Smithsonian Institution

Larry Goldschmidt, Administrative Director, Stewardship of Historic Properties, National Trust for Historic Preservation

Martha Aikens, Superintendent, Mather Employee Development Center, National Park Service

Donn Neal, Executive Director, Society of American Archivists

Melanie Solomon, Student, Cooperstown Graduate Program (Recorder)

Introduction

State and regional organizations seem, on the surface, to be quite similar. We all offer workshops, seminars, and annual meetings for all levels of museum staff on both nuts and bolts topics such as grant writing and exhibition development and on more theoretical issues such as long range planning and advocacy. But when this working group dug beneath the surface, several interesting things emerged.

To use the language of business, state and regional organizations have several distinctive competencies. We are all very close to our consumers and have the freedom and flexibility to respond to the demands of that market quickly. Because we are credible providers, our constituency will generally respond positively to our program innovations. Taken together, this means we are in a position to help to advance professional development in history museums.

Although there is great similarity, there is also specialization within this large universe. As the provider organization gets more localized, the subjects addressed tend to be more practical, the experience level of the participants shifts downward, and the faculty and teaching style is more collegial and less formal.

A wide range of subjects is covered in our programs but there are two glaring gaps in the offerings. There are few examples of successful programs in content areas. And there are not many opportunities to discuss the philosophical underpinnings of our profession in an organized or rigorous way.

Because we have not clearly identified goals for most of these programs, or asked our audience to articulate their goals for participating, we do not have a tangible sense of success. Do people leave our programs really knowing how to do something? Or do they merely have a general sense of how it is done? Given the realities of professional development programs, which is the more realistic goal? The working group shared a sense of frustration with our inability to create programs with sustained involvement by participants.

On the other hand, we can point to some real successes, and the document produced by this group details many of them. We know of collaborative efforts which have brought faculty from academia and other fields together with museum professionals. We identified many unusual formats for programs including longer sessions spread over several months, mentorships, and itinerant workshops. And we found people using new technologies including teleconferencing.

Laura Roberts
Discussion Leader

---

1. Using the OMP Survey and your working knowledge of the field, summarize the current offerings available for history museums in terms of content, audience and level.

__OFFERING__	__OFFERING (cont'd)__	__OFFERING (cont'd)__
There are 9 levels of providers. Their core offerings tend to be similar: workshops, annual meetings	planning.	4. Pairs of states
	2. Regional Associations of Other National Organizations: NPS, ALHFAM, National Trust	5. State associations
		6. Field service organizations in-state agencies
1. AAM Regions. Four of the six have professional staff—potential for more long range, coherent,	3. Standing Professional Committees (SPCs)/ discipline organizations— multi-state	7. Sub-state associations
		8. Metropolitan organizations
		9. Sub-state/metro discipline organizations

CONTENT	AUDIENCE/LEVEL

CONTENT

Mostly museology, which includes both nuts and bolts and more theoretical, issue oriented sessions. The smaller the provider organization, the more nuts and bolts/how-to. What is not well-covered are the philosophical underpinnings ("the big picture") and content (subject area).

1. In the AAM regions, the content is a mix of issues and nuts & bolts. It varies according to audience, constituency of the region and the availability of professional staff. Current hot issues include: the border between the museum and its community; professionalism; integration/communications. Nuts and bolts include: collections; development; exhibitions (media and new technologies).
2. In other regional organizations, the content is a mix of issues and nuts and bolts, often more specifically tailored to less-general membership.
3. SPCs: AAM regions work with Standing Professional Committees to create a balance of content and nuts and bolts training.
4. Pairs of states work together to include states' shared history in their content.
5. State associations offer basically museology training through annual meetings, including panels, pre-meeting workshops, etc.
6. Field service offices often offer one-day workshops that are technical in nature (WI, MN, OH, TX).
7. Sub-state associations: States often have these structures in place that are independent of or collaborate with a state organization to provide training (VA, TX, CA, NY, ID, AZ).
8. Metropolitan organizations are most often consumer-driven in their content. They can address local issues and can be dialogue-oriented because they are close to their audiences (Dallas/Ft. Worth, Houston, many in PA, Chicago).
9. Sub-state disciplinary organizations can examine specific disciplines/museum categories such as education, collections management, art museums, small museums, personnel, directorship, etc. They are very focused and have more periodic informal meetings.

AUDIENCE/LEVEL

Entry level and volunteer staff tend to be reached through local providers. In general, the bigger the organization, the more experienced the participants must be–primarily because of cost.

1. AAM regions serve entry- to senior-level staff with an emphasis on senior level.
2. Other regional organizations serve entry- to mid-level staff (mandated in organizations like the NPS). About 20% of NPS regions do mid-level training.
3. SPCs serve entry- to senior-level staff.
4. Pairs of states serve mid- to senior-level staff.
5. State associations serve entry to senior level staff. Volunteers are best served at the state and sub state level.
6. Field service offices serve entry- to senior-level staff.
7. Sub-state associations serve all staff in their region.
8. Metropolitan associations serve all museum professionals and volunteers in their area.
9. Sub-state disciplinary associations serve their regional constituency, from entry- to mid-level staff plus directors.

2.   Assess the strengths and weaknesses of this group of offerings. Note redundancies, gaps and any other special characteristics.

STRENGTHS

1. Collegiality and diversity of experience:
    Willing to share professional competence and models
    Lack of proprietorship
    Interested in creating networks
2. Market-driven:
    Able to both identify existing markets and create new ones
    Close to the needs of the target markets
    Programming helps raise professional consciousness
3. Flexibility:
    Can act quickly and respond to changes in constituency, economy, and market

WEAKNESSES

1. Responsiveness:
    Hard to really know market
2. Evaluation:
    Difficult to focus objectives and develop accurate measures of success
3. Impact:
    Effort is not sustained and therefore does not effect substantive change
    — Real change takes a lot of time, money and effort: what is the audience's expectation?
4. Quality:
    Insufficient training in educational technique among the professionals with experience to share
5. Diversity:
    Constituencies have different resources, needs, constituencies, preparation
    Geographic disparity
    — Differences in resources
    Geographic differences
    — East/West, etc.
    — Location of resources and constituency

WEAKNESSES (continued)

6. Funding:
    Programs need to be self-supporting
    Outside funding difficult to secure

REDUNDANCIES

1. While offerings must be repeated in every state/region, planning does not need to be
2. "Annual Mentality"—there is a tendency to repeat the same training every year

GAPS

Topical Gaps:
1. Content training—scholarship
2. Philosophy
3. Advocacy
4. Managing change
5. Confronting new realities, managing cutbacks
6. Voluntarism, boards, philanthropy, corporate mergers
7. The big picture, big questions
8. Draw on expertise of other not-for-profits, for-profits, pubic sector

Format Gaps:
1. Dialogue-rather than panels, lectures (one-way learning)
2. Sustained training—Continuing education

3. What attributes and resources does your group of providers bring to potential collaborative training programs?

Offers another perspective, point of view, which balances the program	Access to potential audience for program through mailing lists
Credibility of provider validates the program	Access to outside funding
Administrative expertise, particularly with meeting logistics	Access to meeting sites through membership
Providers of contacts, connections, and knowledge of the market	Coordination of different offerings; elimination of redundancies

4. Are there any restrictions/limitations regarding potential collaboration/partnership efforts that should be noted?

PROS	CONS
Time saving	Too time-consuming
Broadening point of view	Leadership can be amorphous
Saves money	Dilution of focus
Easier to raise money, find underwriting funds	Side-tracked by partners
PR value—exposure	Uneven distribution of benefits
Stretching scarce resources	Competing agendas
Expanding/sharing agendas	
Allows specialization and sharing of specialists	
Doubles audience	
Enhances experience of audience	

5. Has your group of providers been a partner in collaborative training programs? Are there specific successful programs inside or outside the field that we should highlight as models?

SPECIFIC EXAMPLES	SPECIFIC EXAMPLES (continued)
The PA Federation of Museums and Historical Organizations contracted with the PA state agency for history to administer a re-grant program. The program provided money to small, rural or historical agencies which were not currently taking advantage of the state agency's grant program to hire a consultant to teach them the grant writing process.	The Alaska Museums Association has arranged with the Bell Corp. to do infrequent teleconferencing training programs. Distance between museums is thus overcome in an extremely cost-effective way.
	The Arizona State Museum (connected with the University of Arizona), Arizona Central Community College, and the Arizona Com-

mission on the Arts have combined resources to put together a program called T-MAP (Tribal Museums Assessment Program) geared specifically toward tribal museums. ATLATL, a Native American service organization, may be involved as well.

Regional Council of Historical Agencies' New Directors Institute. A 4 1/2 day program for museum directors on the job for less than 2 years. Through roundtable discussions, lectures, and case studies, the program explored areas of concern to directors including their role in fundraising, collections, exhibitions, program development, legal and ethical issues and other areas. The program included 28 participants and a faculty of 8 from New York state. One result of the program has been the creation of an informal network of institute participants who continue to meet at intervals and communicate frequently by phone and mail. Funded by the New York State Council on the Arts.

NPS Interpretive Skills Team is a group of "circuit riders" who provide training (on a variety of interpretive skills) to organizations within the region (NPS and others). Also act as problem-solvers doing on-site diagnosis and consulting and evaluation.

"Culture and Agriculture," an interpretive exhibit apprenticeship, State Historical Society of Wisconsin. The SHSW guided 12 local historical organizations through the process of researching, planning, and producing an exhibit on the diversity of agricultural history in Wisconsin. Each local organization represented a crop or style of agriculture from its area. Under the guidance of the SHSW professional staff, representatives of the local organizations gained experience in conceptual planning, selecting artifacts, writing labels. and fabrication techniques.

"Exhibiting Your Community's Heritage," Instructional videotapes, State Historical Society of Wisconsin. The SHSW produced a series of five instructional videotapes about planning and preparing exhibits. Each program presents a local history exhibit, explains aspects of its interpretive planning such as choosing the topic, selecting artifacts,

or writing label text, and demonstrates fabrication techniques used in the exhibit. An accompanying printed manual summarizes the program content for each instructional tape. The tapes are used by museum associations or field services programs in 17 states.

The Texas Association of Museums (P.O. Box 13353, Austin, TX 78711) will have a field resources program available to its membership and all interested parties by the end of 1990. Data on individuals and institutions and their resources/skills/knowledge available for use will be placed on computer and made available. Individuals listed have agreed to provide assistance without a fee or at cost/expenses. Piloted by the Louisiana Association of Museums. Extended this year to Texas and California.

Collaborative project model: Between association and university continuing education office and university business faculty: Training that brings participants together for intensive, well-focused exploration of a topic and transmission to new techniques, for example, in management skills. They work together in small groups of develop a project for application afterwards back at their museums. Then after implementing or initiating the application of skills learned over a couple of months at their museum, they come together again to report on the progress, evaluate success and impact and problem-solve. During the interim period between training sessions, participants use their small groups for support and peer mentoring. *Virginia Association of Museums.*

OTHER IDEAS

Lending library programs (available through most field service offices)
Self study certification—Ohio
Scholar in residence (on-site)—Week-long: VA Historical Society
Contracting with national organizations for local on-site sessions—South Carolina
Dealing with controversial topics—RCHA

OTHER IDEAS (continued)

OTHER IDEAS (continued)

Interdisciplinary approaches for use on local
    level—RCHA
Humanities committee—Collections evaluation,
    exhibit proposals, grants

Intern programs
Disaster planning training—trains teams of staff.
    Western Museums Conference, consortia in
    central MA

6. Burning Issues

Cross training of museum staffs
The theory and philosophy of our field: Is it
    expanding? Do we work to expand it?
Creative tension *versus* chaos
Dealing with controversial topics
Institutional mission: Where is the emphasis? Is
    there a mission? Should the mission change?
    Mission *versus* political agenda. Should the
    mission be re-evaluated? If so, when?
Being alert to current trends in education and
    society

How many issues should museums take on?
    Priorities
Dealing with disenfranchised groups
Do museums "match" their audiences? Should
    they?
What is the relationship of the museum and the
    community? How can we balance growing
    professionalism and greater community
    access and involvement?

The members of the Training Providers: State and Regional Organizations working group were—

Laura Roberts, Director, New England Museums Association (Discussion Leader)
Jean Cutler, Executive Director, Pennsylvania Federation of Museums and Historical Organizations
Jacqueline Day, Executive Director, Regional Conference of Historical Agencies, NY
Thomas McKay, Coordinator, Local History Office, State Historical Society of Wisconsin
Robert Bluthardt, Chairman, Training Feasibility Committee, Texas Association of Museums
Kathryn Sibley, Executive Coordinator, Western Museums Conference
Edith Whiteman, Executive Director, Virginia Association of Museums
Cynthia Kryston, Chief of Interpretation, National Park Service, North Atlantic Regional Office
Diane Kereluik, Student, Cooperstown Graduate Program (Recorder)

Training Providers: Structured Programs

Introduction

The definition of structured programs adopted for group discussion included degree and certificate granting programs at the graduate level and continuing education programs such as mid career seminars and institutes. Tremendous diversity exists in all types of structured programs. For university based degree programs the variability rests, in part, in the balance between discipline based courses and museum studies classes or in the focus of the degree, for example, historic administration or museum education. The number of requirements and level of quality evident in programs was another area of diversity. In mid career training, the length, focus, audience, and curriculum is as varied as there are offerings. The group noted that the rich variety is on the one hand good, and yet, the consumer needs guidelines from the profession when trying to discern excellence from mediocrity.

The greatest concerns of the group fell into two main areas. The first area is the pressing need for museums to diversify their personnel in order to more accurately reflect our pluralistic nation. This agenda to train, hire and represent multicultural perspectives in our museums increases the pressure on both training programs and the field to respond together. This requires that all types of training demonstrate diversity in their staff, faculty, students, and participants, and that training curricula be reviewed and expanded to broaden the opportunities and ideologies presented in programs.

The second area is the critical need for an expanded foundation of funding, leadership and standards in our museum training programs at all levels. These three factors were viewed as a delicate balance which affects the productivity and health of individual programs as well as the overall state of museum training in structured programs, nationwide. Placing a higher priority on training and assigning higher levels of funding will enable structured programs to participate in the national agenda in a more prominent way. Further, with degree and certificate granting programs and mid career training institutes proliferating, the need for the field to establish standards is greater than ever.

In conclusion, the group emphasized the need for both trainers and museum professional to collaborate on a much broader scale, for the museum field to shape standards for structured programs, and for the leaders of training programs to adopt training models that are responsive to our expanded museum agenda. These issues need to be addressed simultaneously in order to enable our museums to prosper in the future.

Gail Anderson
Discussion Leader

Overview Statement

The group began with extensive discussions on how to format their discussions and they reached two decisions. First, was to approach the questions in a generic manner. The number of available training programs is too extensive to analyze each one separately. Therefore, they considered the questions by looking at all programs as a group. Second, was to divide the programs into two main groups as follows:

1. Degree granting programs or degree programs with a certificate. Subcategories for this group are (1) museum studies programs; (2) other focus programs, such as public history, historical administration, historic preservation, material culture, education, conservation, and exhibits; and (3) discipline based.
2. Continuing education programs. These are seminars, conferences, etc. on a national, regional, or local basis, whether a single day or longer in duration.

1.   Using the OMP Survey and your working knowledge of the field, summarize the current offerings available for history museums in terms of content, audience and level.

When considering the offering, content, or audience level summarizations for either degrees or degrees with certificates, they are to be applied to each individual sub category.

DEGREE OR DEGREE W/ CERTIFICATE

OFFERING

1. Certificate or degree
2. Mandated percentage of content devoted to museum studies or individual discipline

CONTENT

Curriculum Issues
1. Specific field of experience
2. Percent of practicum to experience
3. History (philosophy and functions)
4. Museum management—ethics, law, finance, administration, governance, external affairs, professional standards, marketing
5. Collections management
6. Public programming—interpretation, exhibits, publications, education, media
7. Curatorial and research
8. Evaluation and analytical
9. Professional competencies

AUDIENCE/LEVEL

1. Entry-level or mid-career enhancement, and career change. For undergraduate and graduate (educational and career level).
2. Diverse ethnic/cultural backgrounds.
3. Local and international (origin and geography).
4. Audience need/program focus (goals).

CONTINUING EDUCATION

OFFERING

1. National and local
2. College/university—organization
3. Annual—intermittent
4. Short term and long term

CONTENT

1. General and specific
2. Theoretical and practical
3. Expertise variance (faculty)

AUDIENCE/LEVEL

1. Diversity
2. Highly focused
3. More mature, sense of humor, with experience

2.   Assess the strengths and weaknesses of this group of offerings. Note redundancies, gaps, and any other special characteristics.

The group developed a set of issues that are pertinent to providers and not necessarily to the field as a whole. To put these issues in context, the group identified two major areas. One, that there needs to be an atmosphere in which fiscal resources, leadership and standards are in an equal balance. If one part of this whole is weak, it has an affect on the other two. The fiscal resources are the key driving force here and the one most likely to throw this relationship out of balance. The second is the lack of multi-cultural involvement in the museum field. Here, there is a balance between faculty, students/graduates and professionals. There is a need to increase multi-cultural involvement in all three of these areas. In light of these two concerns, the issues affecting strengths and weaknesses are:

1. Percentage of museum studies versus academics or discipline
2. Range of existing criteria
3. Variety of needs for training versus the variety of programs
4. Dilemma of accreditation
5. Variety of opportunities; no consensus for what is required
6. Theory versus practice
7. Quality of standards for programs, i.e. faculty qualifications, available resources, access to variety of museums and professionals
8. Variety of philosophies and assumptions driving each type of program
9. Nature of affiliation or host organization, i.e. university, association, etc.
10. Audience needs from entry level to mid career (enhancement) to career change
11. Terminology and definitions (interpretation of)

MUSEUM STUDIES AND OTHER DEGREE PROGRAMS

STRENGTHS	WEAKNESSES
1. Responsiveness to field	1. Lack of cultural diversity of faculty, students and alumni
2. Motivated students and faculty	2. Lack of fiscal resources
3. Awareness of standards	3. High staff demands
4. Autonomy of program director	4. Uneven leadership in programs
5. Availability of human resources	5. Lack of standards in the field
6. Linking theoretical and practical	6. Enrollment driven (FTE)
7. Teamwork	7. Absence of career ladders for trainers
8. Bridge building beyond academy	8. Lack of respect and encouragement from field
9. Alumni networks	9. Training too broad
10. Professional networks	10. Autonomy of program director
11. Public service	11. Lack of scholarship in programs and in the field
12. Internships	
13. Cutting edge research and creativity	

DISCIPLINE BASED

STRENGTHS	WEAKNESSES
1. Accepted standards	1. Reluctance to change
2. Theory	2. Lack of practical knowledge
3. Research/scholarship	3. Little contact with museums
4. Publication	4. Lack of interest
	5. Selfish scholarship
	6. Tenure
	7. Weak placement record
	8. Document oriented
	9. No practicum
	10. Bad attitude
	11. Condescension

CONTINUING EDUCATION

STRENGTHS	WEAKNESSES
1. Flexibility (venue, topic)	1. Variance in financial responsibility for attendees
2. Focus on subject	2. Publicity/coordination
3. Faculty expertise	3. Isolation
4. Professional networks	4. Condescension toward returning students
5. Relevance/applicability	
6. Responsive to change	
7. Collegiality	
8. Peer collaboration	

3.   What attributes and resources does your group of providers bring to potential collaborative training programs?

1. Current scholarship	4. Alumni pool
2. Culling and updating field publications	5. Clearinghouse for information
3. Teaching	6. Developed curriculum

4.   Are there any new challenges regarding potential collaboration/partnership efforts that should be noted?

1. Bring together providers and consumers (multi-cultural)
2. Seek out requisite resources
3. Overcome logistics and competition
4. Assist in overcoming bureaucracy/inertia
5. Foster cross fertilization between museum programs and new audiences
6. Develop corporate partnerships

5.   (A)Has your group of providers been a partner in collaborative training programs? (B)Are there specific successful programs inside or outside the field that we should highlight as models?

A. Yes. On individual, program and organizational basis

B. Successful Models
1. Scholars in residence
2. Corporate support
3. Graduate program and regional/national organizations co-sponsoring programs and projects
4. Adjunct faculty and guest speakers from the field teaching in programs
5. Advisory boards of museum professionals and experts
6. Cooperative projects for exhibits, educational programs, collections management, marketing, etc., between museums and graduate students
7. Internships
8. Government support for projects and programs
9. Housing literature and resources of programs and associations in one facility

The Members of the Training Providers: Structured Programs working group were—

Gail Anderson, Director, Center for Museum Studies, John F. Kennedy University (Discussion Leader)
Barbara Howe, Director, Public History Program, West Virginia University
James Huhta, Director, Center for Historic Preservation, Middle Tennessee State University
Peggy Howells, Administrator, Museum Studies, Colonial Williamsburg, Seminar for Historical Administration
Bryant Tolles, Director, Museum Studies Program, University of Delaware
Langdon Wright, Associate Professor and Director of Admissions, Cooperstown Graduate Program
Thomas Ellig, Student, Cooperstown Graduate Program (Recorder)

WORKING GROUP REPORTS
TRAINING CONSUMERS

Administration
Collections
Exhibits
Education and Interpretation
Research and Scholarship
Small Museums

Training Consumers: Administration

Introduction

The working group responsible for examining the needs of future museum administrators looked at the requirements of our task and decided that the words *knowledge* and *skills* needed to be defined. *Knowledge* was defined as that body or group of information needed to perform a job. *Skills* were defined as one's ability to use knowledge effectively in his or her day to day routine. Further, the group felt it necessary to develop a matrix. It determined that administration performed certain "functions" and that knowledge and skills were necessary to perform each function.

Eventually, nine administrative functions were identified. They were: security and maintenance of facilities, fund-raising, governance, financial management, planning (especially for change), institutional marketing, programs—and, most importantly, personnel. The group felt that certain knowledge and different skills were needed in each functional area.

Several common skills repeated themselves. The most common was communication. Another was leadership. Negotiation and evaluation were other skills necessary to being successful in an administrative capacity.

In question four, the group struggled with the question of proper training. In our report we felt that the "knowledge/skill" that we listed in question three were essential. "Content considerations" were limited to ALI-ABA type models, or 1-2 week in-depth seminars for advanced professionals, or four year undergraduate programs aimed at a graduate specialization. The student report disagrees with this finding with the comment that "this lacks the opportunity for academic background." The panel felt that the four year program could set up a general academic program leading to more intensive specialization as the student progressed through the four years and on to graduate school. Management seminars need to be increased in quantity and quality for mid-career and advanced level professionals. Logistical considerations continue to be time and money.

Salvatore G. Cilella, Jr.
Discussion Leader

---

1. Articulate the knowledge and skills necessary to do the particular job in history museums suggested by your group's title.

KNOWLEDGE

General
    Organizational structure
    Organizational behavior
    Legal
    Evaluation of personnel
    Compensation and benefits
    Administration
Security and maintenance of facilities
    Electronics and related systems
    Training of personnel
    Disaster preparedness
    Legal
    Audience
    Environment

KNOWLEDGE (continued)

    Construction, architecture, contracting
        (renovation, new building, expansion)
Fund-raising
    Legal
    Funding sources, strategies, tools and costs
    Knowledge of the community and competition
    Resources (internal and external)
    Museum mission, program and goals
Governance
    Legislative process and systems and lobbyists
    Different models for governance
    Ethics

Community	Security and maintenance of facilities
Mission	Construction management, negotiations, bids and purchases
Financial management	Facility management (plumbing, carpentry, electricity, janitorial services, etc.)
Finance	Communication
Computer use	Fund-raising
Investment	Organizational
Insurance	Solicitation, cultivation and recognition of donors and trustees
Earned income	Communication (written and oral)
Licensing	Grantsmanship
Planning for change	Governance
Planning process and resources	Communication
Evaluation	Management of trustees
Assessment and history of the institution and community	Administration of volunteers
Change (how it works, how to effect change)	Financial
Institutional marketing	Planning
Marketing (what it is)	Cost analysis
Ethics	Budget administration
The market, the product	Planning for change
Media: how to use it for different audiences	Organization
The five "P"s (Price, Product, People, Positioning, Promotion)	Communication
Programs	Leadership

KNOWLEDGE (continued)

Community
Mission
Financial management
    Finance
    Computer use
    Investment
    Insurance
    Earned income
    Licensing
Planning for change
    Planning process and resources
    Evaluation
    Assessment and history of the institution and
        community
    Change (how it works, how to effect change)
Institutional marketing
    Marketing (what it is)
    Ethics
    The market, the product
    Media: how to use it for different audiences
    The five "P"s (Price, Product, People, Positioning, Promotion)
Programs
    Collections, education, research, exhibits, conservation
    Standards
    Project or team projects
Personnel
    Communication: interviews, evaluation, memos
    Orientation to jobs
    Recruiting
    Retention of employees
    Training: continuing education
Student Input:
    Management theory
    Understanding of all museum operations and of the jobs of all museum personnel
    Museum ethics as stated by AAM/ICOM
    Security and maintenance for collections
    Security and maintenance for physical plant
    Occupational health and safety
    Laws affecting museums, including:
        Tax laws
        Property laws
        Employment practice laws
        Etc.
Awareness of opportunities to collaborate with other cultural institutions

SKILLS

Security and maintenance of facilities
    Construction management, negotiations, bids and purchases
    Facility management (plumbing, carpentry, electricity, janitorial services, etc.)
    Communication
Fund-raising
    Organizational
    Solicitation, cultivation and recognition of donors and trustees
    Communication (written and oral)
    Grantsmanship
Governance
    Communication
    Management of trustees
    Administration of volunteers
Financial
    Planning
    Cost analysis
    Budget administration
Planning for change
    Organization
    Communication
    Leadership
    Negotiation
    Evaluation
Institutional marketing
    Communication
Programs
    Leadership (convey the vision)
Student Input:
    Interpersonal/management skills: getting along with board, community, and staff

2. Place the knowledge and skills in priority order according to: (1) basic and/or essential, (2) useful but not essential, (3) increasingly more important.

BASIC AND/OR ESSENTIAL	USEFUL BUT NOT ESSENTIAL	INCREASINGLY MORE IMPORTANT
Personnel	Construction management	Marketing
Security and maintenance of facilities	Management of volunteers	Computer applications
Fund-raising	Recruitment techniques	Legislative issues
Governance	Licensing and copyrights	Grantsmanship
Financial management	Legislative process	Management of trustees
Planning (basics)	Investments	Training and retention of personnel
Planning strategies		Financial management
Institutional marketing		Knowledge of competition
Programs		Investment strategy
Communications		Fund-raising
Time management		Program evaluation
Leadership		Earned income
Earned income		Disaster planning
Evaluation of programs		Planning for change
Audience assessment		*Student Input:*
Student Input:		Management theory
Ethics		Awareness of opportunities to collaborate with other cultural institutions
Knowledge of museum-related laws		
Management skills		
Knowledge of all museum operations and jobs		
Occupational health and safety		
Security and maintenance for collections		
Security and maintenance for physical plant		

3.   Organize the knowledge and skills as to whether they are necessary for entry into the field or for work in mid/advanced career positions.

ENTRY LEVEL/NEW TO THE FIELD	MID/ADVANCED CAREER POSITIONS
501(c)(3)	Personnel/compensation/benefits
Legal: constitution and by-laws	Licensing
Security and maintenance of facilities	Strategic planning
Fund-raising	Management of volunteers
Governance	Recruitment techniques
Financial management	Licensing and copyrights
Planning (basics)	Legislative process
Planning strategies	Investments
Institutional marketing	Marketing
Programs	Computer applications
Communications	Legislative issues
Time management	Grantsmanship
Leadership	Management of trustees
Earned income	Training and retention of personnel
Evaluation of programs	Financial management
Audience assessment	Knowledge of competition
Student Input:	Investment strategy
Personnel/compensation/benefits	Fund-raising
Personnel management	Program evaluation
Grant writing	Earned income
Computer applications	Disaster planning
Ethics	Planning for change
Management skills	*Student Input:*
Understanding of all museum operations and of	Awareness of opportunities to collaborate with
the jobs of all museum personnel	other cultural institutions
Security and maintenance for collections	Management theory
Security and maintenance for physical plant	(Knowledge of competition–what does this
Occupational health and safety	mean? Competition for funding sources,
Laws affecting museums	audience/tourism, or personnel?)
Fundraising	

4.   Given the list of knowledge and skills the group has identified, what type(s) of training offerings will provide adequate coverage?

KNOWLEDGE/SKILL

All skills and knowledge listed above in question 3

CONTENT CONSIDERATIONS

ALI-ABA model: schools of specialized training (compare them to medical training and specialization, but do not disregard a broad spectrum of training)

One- to two-week schools on each skill and knowledge area

At above schools, break out or define levels of experience, knowledge and skills

Four-year undergraduate program in general museum studies, then specialize in graduate school

Graduate work with co-op studies program in a specialty

Student Input:

Management seminars

Financial management courses in graduate programs

Museum graduate programs

(We disagree with 4-year undergraduate program in general museum studies. This lacks the opportunity for academic background. Museum studies students need a background in an academic discipline. We prefer the specific subject content (history, sociology, education, computer science, graphic arts, etc.) in undergraduate school and general museum studies at the graduate level.

LOGISTICAL CONSIDERATIONS

Time

Money in budget

Scholarships for meeting attendance

Exchange programs

Geographical location: so all have a chance to attend

Student Input:

Make training accessible to people with families (for example, provide day care)

Make training available to people with disabilities

People sensitivity issues should affect the design of a training course: Make training environment nurturing and respectful of people as individuals

5.   In the spirit of being true "consumers," are there any other burning issues on your minds relating to professional training? If so, please articulate them, and note why you think these are issues requiring timely consideration.

Communications: calendar of training events (possible using programs available in cultural fields other then the museum field)

Standards: guidelines for educational programs (college and museum taught) and for museum studies courses and programs

IRS and new laws: deductability of contributions/UBIT

Repatriation

Ethics of marketing and fund-raising

Employer/employee relations

Student Input:

More opportunities for undergraduate museum courses, but not necessarily undergraduate museum majors

We think there should be more financial assistance from the employing institution for further training, including seminars and degree programs

Museum management styles need to keep changing to keep pace with changing management styles in the for-profit sector

The members of the Training Consumers: Administration working group were—

Salvatore Cilella, Director, Columbia Museum, SC (Discussion Leader)
Amina Dickerson, Director of Education and Public Programs, Chicago Historical Society
Alice Knierim, Division Head, Museum and Educational Programs, State of Alabama Department of Archives and
*   History*
Wilson O'Donnell, Director, New Jersey Historical Society
Jean Svadlenak, Consultant, Kansas City, MO
George Seeley, Student, Cooperstown Graduate Program (Recorder)

Introduction

Collections have always been central to the work of museums. The interpretation of material culture is what sets museums apart from schools, libraries and other educational institutions. Perhaps no area of museum work has changed as much as that dealing with collections. The traditional role of curator has changed with the addition of collections managers, guest scholars and museum educators. The Collections Working Group began by acknowledging that an institution's mission is driven by a balance between collections, ideas, and audience. Within this framework we identified the following body of knowledge we believe collections professionals must have in order to effectively acquire, care for, exhibit and interpret their collections.

Susan Page Tillett
Discussion Leader

1. Articulate the knowledge and skills necessary to do the particular job in history museums suggested by your group's title.

KNOWLEDGE

I. Knowledge: Museum Profession
   A. Principles of museum work including:
      1. An understanding of ethics
      2. An understanding of the principles of collections management
      3. An understanding of various museum operations
      4. An understanding of individual roles of various museum professionals
   B. Understanding of the roles of museums in society and the history of museums
   C. Knowledge of current scholarship and research sources
II. Knowledge: Collections Management
   A. Object care and handling
      1. Conservation
      2. Collections monitoring
      3. Storage
      4. Moving and shipping
      5. Accessibility to the physical collection
      6. Display
      7. Security
   B. Documentation
      1. Systems and standards
      2. Accessing information
   C. Knowledge of current scholarship
      1. Field work studies

KNOWLEDGE (continued)

      2. Material culture studies
      3. Social history studies
      4. Trends in historiography
III. Knowledge: Interpreting Collections
   A. Audience awareness
      1. Knowledge of audience
      2. Understanding of audience needs

SKILLS

I. Skills: Museum Profession
   A. Management skills
      1. Project management
      2. Planning
      3. Teamwork
      4. Budget planning
      5. Human resources management
      6. Flexibility
   B. Ability to access current scholarship and research sources
II. Skills: Collections Management
   A. Care and handling
   B. Documentation
      1. Cataloging
      2. Use of documentation systems
      3. Analysis of documentation systems
      4. Database management
      5. Photography

SKILLS (continued)	SKILLS (continued)

C. Mastery of research methods including accessing material culture studies, field studies, and social history sources
D. Ability and desire to serve actively as collections advocates
III. Skills: Collections Interpretation
   A. Exhibition production skills
	B. Artifact fluency
	   1. The ability to communicate understanding of artifacts
	   2. Ability to interpret artifacts
	C. Research methodology
	D. Writing
	E. Verbal communication

2. Place the knowledge and skills in priority order according to: (1) basic and/or essential, (2) useful but not essential, (3) increasingly more important.

BASIC AND/OR ESSENTIAL	USEFUL BUT NOT ESSENTIAL	INCREASINGLY MORE IMPORTANT
An understanding that an institution's mission is driven by a balance of collections, ideas, and audience Collections advocacy Artifact literacy Knowledge of care and handling Documentation knowledge and skills Knowledge of museum work Artifact interpretation skills Exhibit production skills Knowledge and skills with regard to current research sources and techniques Management skills An understanding of the roles and history of museums	Ability to use current collections technology Experience Willingness to share/communicate individual knowledge	Management skills An understanding of technology (computers, HVAC systems, photocopiers, *et al.*) Crisis preparedness and management

3. Organize the knowledge and skills as to whether they are necessary for entry into the field or for work in mid/advanced career positions.

ENTRY LEVEL/NEW TO THE FIELD	MID/ADVANCED CAREER POSITIONS
Knowledge of the mission and principles of museum work	Understanding roles and history of museums
Knowledge of proper care and handling techniques	Mastery of management skills
Knowledge of standards of documentation	Skill in care and handling
Mastery of research methods	Skill in applying standards of documentation
Artifact literacy	Artifact fluency
Collections advocacy	Continued collections advocacy
Ability to work as part of a team	Subject matter specialty
Understanding the roles and history of museums	Exhibition techniques
Computer literacy	Mastery of communication techniques

4. Given the list of knowledge and skills the group has identified, what type(s) of training offerings will provide adequate coverage?

KNOWLEDGE/SKILLS

I. Entry Level Training Offerings
   A. Undergraduate level knowledge and scholarship
   B. Graduate level Museum Studies programs
II. Mid Career Training Offerings
   A. Management skills
   B. Care and handling skills
   C. Collections documentation

CONTENT CONSIDERATIONS

I. Entry Level
   A. Preparation at this level should be in an

CONTENT (continued)

academic discipline; Museum Studies should not be taught as an undergraduate major
   B. The collections working group embraces the AAM Museum Studies Committee recommendations concerning Museum Studies program content
II. Mid Career/Advanced
   A. Training should include situational problem-solving geared toward collections and effective teamwork strategies
   B. Content should focus on confirmation of current practices and

CONTENT (continued)

updating professionals with regard to current practices
   C. Content should be based on nationally accepted models for documentation in general, programs for technological literacy, and programs on library information management
   D. Content should focus on a discussion of criteria for collecting
   E. Content should be based on individual needs and should be institutionally sponsored in terms of the provision of resources
   F. Content should be based on individual

CONTENT (continued)	LOGISTICS (continued)	LOGISTICS (continued)

needs but should include such subjects as program evaluation techniques, program testing techniques, and approaches to team-work in program design and exhibit production
 	
## LOGISTICAL CONSIDERATIONS 	
 	
I. Entry Level
  A. Undergraduate liberal arts degree or equivalent experience
  B. Master of Arts degree earned through Museum Studies program or in academic major with
	Museum Studies exposure (certificate)
	II. Mid/Advanced Level
	  A. Museum Management Institute Model or Kellogg Program Model would be appropriate logistically
	  B. A variety of training experiences would be appropriate logistically including:
	    1. The AASLH/ National Park Service Model of a 3-5 day intensive program
	    2. A program using non-print media such as a video telecourse
	  C. A variety of frameworks for training
		would be appropriate including newsletters, seminars, university courses in theory and technique
		  D. A variety of approaches to training would be appropriate including but not limited to issue related seminars and conferences
		  E. Various logistical approaches would be appropriate; training should be based on individual needs

5.   In the spirit of being true "consumers," are there any other burning issues on your minds relating to professional training? If so, please articulate them, and note why you think these are issues requiring timely consideration.

The collections working group identified a number of burning issues including:

1. The need to preserve the diversity of training now available
2. The importance of role definitions for collections professionals
3. The shifting position of collections in relationship to mission, ideas, and audience
4. The issue of the importance of cultural diversity including:
  A. Issues related to repatriation

  B. Recruitment of minorities to museum studies programs
  C. The importance of addressing the intellectual diversity of audiences
  D. The importance of broadening minority representation on boards in order to foster sensitivity to cultural issues
5. The importance of downsizing and resource management
6. Museums should make use of existing training programs in other disciplines where appropriate

The members of the Training Consumers: Collections working group were—

Susan Tillett, Director of Curatorial Affairs, Chicago Historical Society (Discussion Leader)
Mary Case, Director, Office of the Registrar, Smithsonian Institution
Lynn Harlan, Museum Technician, National Museum of American History
Frank McKelvey, Consultant, Wilmington, DE
Jane Spillman, Curator of American Glass, Corning Museum of American Glass
Johanna Metzgar, Student, Cooperstown Graduate Program (Recorder)

Introduction

The Exhibits Working Group approached the requirements of exhibit work as a product or process rather than as the knowledge and skills of an individual. We all agreed that exhibit work was by definition interdisciplinary. A number of tensions and juxtapositions kept recurring in our discussions related to the interdisciplinary nature of exhibits and are probably worth mentioning. They are: generalist *versus* specialist; staff *versus* consultants; and individual *versus* team authorship and responsibility. We decided to organize our comments on the basis of the major categories of knowledge and skills that relate to exhibition work: history/content; material culture/objects; design/communication; audience/education; and management. Throughout our discussions of these areas the subject of vision

and leadership was a particular concern as was cultural diversity in museums. Distinctions between entry and mid-career skills brought up interesting insights into how people progress. It became apparent that the broader the responsibilities of a supervisor, the more important it was that the person have a knowledge of the total process. In thinking about how people acquire these skills, we tried to be as inclusive as possible and to suggest ways that people acquire content as well as practical skills. We also made an effort to suggest that content information for exhibitions is often acquired by non-traditional research techniques.

Barbara Franco
Discussion Leader

1.   Articulate the knowledge and skills necessary to do the particular job in history museums suggested by your group's title.

KNOWLEDGE	SKILLS
History/content	Research, interpretation, writing Conceptual framework Non-traditional research and collecting (e.g. oral history)
Design/communication	3-D, 2-D Technical Fabrication/production Aesthetic Function Technology Conceptual framework
Material culture/objects	Conservation Object handling Research and interpretation Writing

KNOWLEDGE (continued)	SKILLS (continued)
Education/audience	Learning styles/educational theory Evaluation Expectations Behavior
Management	Leadership Goal setting Organization Problem solving
Vision	
Understanding of overall process and final product	

2.   Place the knowledge and skills in priority order according to: (1) basic and/or essential, (2) useful but not essential, (3) increasingly more important.

BASIC AND/OR ESSENTIAL	USEFUL BUT NOT ESSENTIAL	INCREASINGLY MORE IMPORTANT

Historical content
Design/communication
Objects
Audience
Vision/goal setting
Management
Conceptual framework
Leadership
Conservation
Writing
	Fiscal management
	Grantsmanship
	Public relations
	Publications
		Educational theory
		Evaluation
		Technology
		Conservation
		   –Develop more skills
		Management
		   –Teams/models of organi-
		    zation

3.   Organize the knowledge and skills as to whether they are necessary for entry into the field or for work in mid/advanced career positions.

ENTRY LEVEL/NEW TO THE FIELD

Grounding in specific discipline
  –Design
  –History
  –Material culture
  –Education
Familiarity with exhibit process as a collaborative, interdisciplinary vehicle
Knowledge of museums as public educational institutions (past and present) that collect, preserve, and interpret
Communication skills

MID/ADVANCED CAREER POSITIONS

Increased proficiency in subject specialty and working knowledge of other disciplines
  –Visual communication
  –Learning styles
  –Historical methodology
Awareness and understanding of collections management issues

MID/ADVANCED CAREER (continued)

Ability to create and articulate a conceptual framework
Setting and implementing goals and objectives
  –Immediate and long range
Leadership and vision
Effective communication
Resource management
  –People
  –Fiscal
Knowledge of exhibit philosophy and methodologies, and the ability to choose and implement them appropriately
Evaluation
  –Self
  –Staff
  –Institution
  –Audience
  –Community
  –Society

4.   Given the list of knowledge and skills the group has identified, what type(s) of training offerings will provide adequate coverage?

KNOWLEDGE/SKILL	CONTENT CONSIDERATIONS	LOGISTICAL CONSIDERATIONS
History/content	University faculty	Degree programs
Research, interpretation	Museum professionals	Individual courses
	Community leaders	Seminars
	Independent scholars	Visiting scholars
	Historical societies and museums	Staff development
		Reading lists
		Oral history
		Video

KNOWLEDGE/SKILL (continued)	CONTENT (continued)	LOGISTICS (continued)
Design/communication	University faculty Designers and artists Museum professionals Journals Marketing personnel Social sciences professionals	Degree programs Internships Project related seminars Criticism and review Other exhibits
Curatorial Objects and their care	University faculty Museum professionals Community leaders Independent scholars Collectors Manufacturers Historical societies and museums Conservators	Degree program (e.g. Material Culture, Decorative Arts, Art History, History of Technology) Internships Seminars Reading lists Visiting scholars Audio-visual Consultations
Education/audience	Community University faculty Teachers Marketing personnel Social sciences personnel Consultants Audience	Degree programs Evaluation surveys Focus groups Seminars
Management	Business leaders University faculty (including business) Museum professionals Community leaders Lawyers	Degree programs Seminars Workshops Current literature
Technology	Manufacturers Specialists Scholars	Degree programs Seminars and courses On-the-job training Audio-visual Consultations Conferences

5. In the spirit of being true "consumers," are there any other burning issues on your minds relating to professional training? If so, please articulate them, and note why you think these are issues requiring timely consideration.

Conceptual frameworks to do exhibits
Outside consultant *versus* in-house designer
Authorship
    –Individual
    –Institution
Exhibit reviews
    –Authorship/credit/responsibility
Lifelong learning/continuing education
Censorship
Generalists *versus* specialists
Various process models
    –Teams
    –Individuals

Technology
Exhibits methodology
Leadership
Balance of ideas and objects
Museum and it's community
Cultural diversity
    –Recruitment
    –Collections
Issues of safety arising from the use of dangerous
    chemicals and tools in exhibit construction

The members of the Training Consumers: Exhibits working group were—

Barbara Franco, Assistant Director, The Museum of Our National Heritage (Discussion Leader)
Lonnie Bunch, Curator, National Museum of American History
Richard Chavka, Managing Director, Mount Lebanon Shaker Village
Deborah Kmetz, Local History Specialist, State Historical Society of Wisconsin
Pamela Myers, Head, Exhibitions and Building Services, Museum of the City of New York
Helen Psarakis, Student, Cooperstown Graduate Program (Recorder)

Training Consumers: Education and Interpretation

Introduction

Our group quickly defined what educators need to know: their subject, their audience, how to teach and how to manage their programs and people. Yet, we kept coming back to the intangible and immeasurable components of what makes a good educator–a love of history and a desire to communicate human understanding through his or her teaching and creativity. Those components are included too, but we decided not to pursue ways of training for these qualities. On the second question, we defined entry level as those positions where implementation is the main responsibility. Mid-career and advanced was used to describe jobs where program development and management were the most impor-

tant functions. We all noted the irony of the typical museum education career–that of an excellent program presenter or developer rewarded by being thrust into a management position because that is the only method of career advancement. Finally, the group noted that as museums become more client-centered, the education and interpretation functions are becoming more central, exerting pressure on those staff members to increase their knowledge about the audience and learning in the museum for all groups. Now, more than ever, educators need good mid career training.

Elizabeth Sharpe
Discussion Leader

---

1. Articulate the knowledge and skills necessary to do the particular job in history museums suggested by your group's title.

KNOWLEDGE/SKILLS

I. History, Material Culture
    A. Content information
        –Basic
        –Particular
    B. Interdisciplinary awareness
    C. History of museums and museum interpretation
    D. Interest in, love for history and its role in human understanding
    E. Skill in performing historic activities
    F. Analysis, interpretation
        –Basic
        –Particular
    G. Research
        –Basic
        –Particular
    H. Artifact interpretation
        –Basic
        –Particular
II. Audience and Teaching Methods
    A. Learning theory and learning styles

KNOWLEDGE/SKILLS (continued)

    B. Knowledge of community needs and issues
        –Attitudes, emotions
        –Social, economic, political issues
        –Demographics (museum and local)
        –Class, cultural diversity
    C. Varied audiences
        –Intergenerational
        –Disabilities
        –Age
        –Gender
    D. Audience research
        –Evaluation methods
        –Evaluation literature
    E. Visitor behavior in exhibits
        –Reading levels
    F. Academic community
    G. Teaching experience
    H. Successful communication with audiences

I. Presentation
    –Write objectives, set goals
    –Voice and diction
    –Body language
    –Eye contact
    –Listening
    –Questioning strategies
    –Choose appropriate materials
    –Types of presentation
    –Organization
    –Adaptability, flexibility
    –Sense of humor
    –Presenting sensitive issues
J. Design, development, and implementation of programs (tours, performing arts, etc.)
    –Discovery rooms
    –Exhibits
    –Interactives
    –Publications
    –Curriculum
    –Presenting sensitive issues
K. Work with outside consultants
L. Teaching interpreters, docents to teach
M. Creativity
N. External resources

III. Administration
A. Ethics
    –Personal
    –Professional
    –Community
B. Technical (A/V, computers)

C. Management
    –Personnel
        –Interviewing, hiring
        –Evaluation
        –Staff development, coaching, rewarding
        –Leadership
        –Expanding staff, professional diversity
        –Employee and professional counseling, referral
    –Goal setting and maintenance
    –Financial
    –Legal issues
    –Teamwork
    –Conflict resolution, negotiation
    –Networking
D. Academic and business communities and government
E. Long-range planning
F. Educational system (national, state, local)
    –Players
    –Issues, pressures
    –Systems
    –Curriculum
G. General understanding of all other museum functions
H. Communication
    –Oral
    –Written
I. Marketing and public relations

2.   Place the knowledge and skills in priority order according to: (1) basic and/or essential, (2) useful but not essential, (3) increasingly more important.

BASIC AND/OR ESSENTIAL

Historical content information
Analysis/interpretation skills
Research skills–basic
Artifact interpretation–basic
How to look at the past
History of museums and museum education/
    interpretation
Interest in/love for history and its role in human
    understanding
Learning theory
Teaching experience
Knowledge of community, successful communi-
    cation
Presentation
Audience research
Knowledge of varied audiences
Design, development, implementation
Ethics
Other museum functions
Management
Critical thinking/information management
Teamwork
Creative thinking
Oral and written communication

USEFUL BUT NOT ESSENTIAL

Historical content information–particular
Analysis/interpretation skills–particular
Research skills–particular
Artifact interpretation–particular
Knowledge of academic and business communi-
    ties and government networking
Knowledge of educational system
Technical knowledge and skills

INCREASINGLY MORE IMPORTANT

Interdisciplinary awareness
Visitors in exhibits
Audience research
Knowledge of varied audiences
Work with outside consultants
Long-range planning

3.   Organize the knowledge and skills as to whether they are necessary for entry into the field or for work in mid/advanced career positions.

ENTRY LEVEL/NEW TO THE FIELD

Historical content information–basic
Analysis/interpretation skills–basic
Research skills–basic
Artifact interpretation–basic
How to look at the past
History of museums and museum education,
    interpretation
Interest in/love for history and its role in human
    understanding
Learning theory
Knowledge of varied audiences

MID/ADVANCED CAREER POSITIONS

Historical content information–particular
Analysis/interpretation skills–particular
Research skills–particular
Artifact interpretation–particular
Interdisciplinary awareness
Knowledge of community needs and issues
Visitors in exhibits
Audience research
Knowledge of academic community
Work with outside consultants
Design/development/implementation

ENTRY LEVEL/NEW TO THE FIELD (continued)	MID/ADVANCED CAREER POSITIONS (continued)
Teaching experience Presentation skills Ethics Technical information/skills Writing/editing Critical thinking, information management Teamwork Creative thinking	Knowledge of academic and business communities and government Networking Knowledge of other museum functions Long-range planning Knowledge of educational system Technical information/skills Management

4.   Given the list of knowledge and skills the group has identified, what type(s) of training offerings will provide adequate coverage?

KNOWLEDGE/ SKILL	CONTENT CONSIDERATIONS	LOGISTICAL CONSIDERATIONS
Presentation	Outside field Inside field	Intensive introduction Incremental (learn, practice, evaluate) Pre-entry and on the job
Historical content	Academia Staff sharing Interdisciplinary experts Community experts	Research leaves Sabbaticals Independent studies Field trips Summer sessions Training within museums
Learning theory	Academia Staff sharing Interdisciplinary experts Community experts	Research leaves Sabbaticals Independent studies Field trips Summer sessions Training within museums
Community/audience needs	Community-based agencies and programs Advisory committees Government agencies Outside experts	Course with practicum Observation/field work

KNOWLEDGE/SKILL (continued)	CONTENT (continued)	LOGISTICS (continued)
Museum audience research	Academia Staff sharing Community experts Museum professionals	Course with practicum Observation/fieldwork
Knowledge of varied audi-	Academia Staff sharing Community experts Museum professionals	Course with practicum Observation/fieldwork
Design/development/inter- pretation	Museum professionals Outside professionals–theater, architecture, computer, video, teaching	Observation of other sites/ programs Internships/residencies Seminars
Ethics	Museum professionals (indi- viduals and organizations) Attorneys Financial advisors	Practica/case studies
Other museum functions	In-house staff Outside professionals	Management tapes Courses
Long-range planning	Outside consultants and museum professionals In-house staff	Incremental in-house Outside seminars Ongoing training
Management	Local business people Museum professionals Management consultants	Management tapes, courses, seminars Skill practice Residencies/internships Case studies Practica

5. In the spirit of being true "consumers," are there any other burning issues on your minds relating to professional training? If so, please articulate them, and note why you think these are issues requiring timely consideration.

–Evaluation and audience research
–Cultural diversity–who are the keepers and interpreters?
–Changing demographics:
    –Age
    –Language/literacy
    –Cultural
    –Family makeup
–Leadership–how will we prepare for:
    –Personal

–Organizations–what is museums' role in bringing social responsibility issues to the fore?
–Vision
–Training–we need:
    –Release time for professional development
    –Money with which to be trained
    –Training to be expected and ongoing (planned)

The members of the Training Consumers: Education and Interpretation working group were—

Elizabeth Sharpe, Deputy Assistant Director for Public Programs, National Museum of American History (Discussion Leader)
Rex Ellis, Director of African American Interpretation and Presentations, Colonial Williamsburg
Marie Hewett, Vice President of Education, Strong Museum
Cynthia Little, Education Director, Historical Society of Pennsylvania
Bart Roselli, Assistant Director for Museum Programs, Historical Society of Western Pennsylvania
Sherill Hatch, Student, Cooperstown Graduate Program (Recorder)

Training Consumers: Research and Scholarship

Introduction

The working group assigned to "Training Consumers: Research and Scholarship" based its conclusions on two presumptions. First, we defined research as having an external product. In a museum setting, such products include exhibitions, publications, lectures, school lessons, family programs, performance scripts, collection catalogues, interpreter training manuals, evaluation questionnaires, and many other applications. Our working group begged the question of whether scholarship for its own sake is or should be an expected function of museums. For the purposes of our assignment, the following lists of skills and priorities assume that the researcher is working on a project with defined objectives and outcomes.

Second, we assumed that the researcher/scholar is working in a museum with a minimal level of resources. Our working group did not define that level, but we acknowledged that adequate time, money, and staffing are prerequisites to accomplish good scholarship. For those without that minimal level the task becomes much more difficult, but lack of resources should not release the small institution from the obligation of making the attempt to produce a quality product.

If one issue could be singled out as a consistent theme for the weekend, it was the idea of inclusiveness. Our working group was no exception, devoting more of our time to this point than to any other. Although our discussions appear in the report as three short sentences under "Burning Issues," readers should know that the working group members were strong advocates. We believe that researchers need to be culturally sensitive, to have an interdisciplinary consciousness, and to acquire humanistic and holistic knowledge. We believe that museums, through research, can be the agencies that will supply much of what has been previously omitted in many areas of scholarship.

Deborah Smith
Discussion Leader

---

1. Articulate the knowledge and skills necessary to do the particular job in history museums suggested by your group's title.

KNOWLEDGE

The products of research and those engaged in research should demonstrate *knowledge* of:
- The connections between objects and ideas
- The institution's mission, audiences, operations
- Cultural sensitivity
- Disciplinary content (the museum's area of specialty)
- Other methodological approaches that can illuminate the museum's area of specialty: (open ended list): archaeology, bibliography, anthropology, historiography, material culture, education, folklore, sociology, psychology, natural science, etc.
- Resources in other museums or the field of

SKILLS

Those engaged in research should demonstrate *skills* in:
- Critical thinking: conceptualization, synthesis, communication
- Organization
- Technology use (data bases, photography, recording, word processing)–or have access to resources with the needed skills
- Exhibition (spatial conceptions, ability to communicate ideas visually)
- Ability to "read" objects, connoisseurship
- Programming skills (awareness of "interactive" learning, composition, and abilities of intended audiences)

KNOWLEDGE (continued)	SKILLS (continued)
research (collections, exhibitions, resource people) and/or the field of research –A graduate degree	–Lifelong learning, continuing education –Mentoring, both as a teacher and student –Collaboration, "team" ability

2.   Place the knowledge and skills in priority order according to 1) basic and/or essential, 2) useful but not essential, 3) increasingly more important.

BASIC AND/OR ESSENTIAL	USEFUL BUT NOT ESSENTIAL	INCREASINGLY MORE IMPORTANT

Knowledge:
   –The connections between objects and ideas
   –The institution's mission, audiences, operations
   –Cultural sensitivity
   –Disciplinary content (the museum's area of specialty)
   –Other methodological approaches that can illuminate the museum's area of specialty: (open ended list): archaeology, bibliography, anthropology, historiography, material culture, education, folklore, sociology, psychology, natural science, etc.
Skills:
   –Critical thinking: conceptualization, synthesis, communication
	Knowledge:
	   –Resources in other museums or the field of research (collections, exhibitions, resource people) and/or the field of research
	Skills:
	   –Organization
	   –Technology use (data bases, photography, recording, word processing)–or have access to resources with the needed skills
	   –Exhibition (spatial conceptions, ability to communicate ideas visually)
	   –Ability to "read" objects, connoisseurship
		Knowledge:
		   –A graduate degree
		Skills:
		   –Programming skills (awareness of "interactive" learning, composition, and abilities of intended audiences)
		   –Lifelong learning, continuing education
		   –Mentoring, both as a teacher and student
		   –Collaboration, "team" ability

3. Organize the knowledge and skills as to whether they are necessary for entry into the field or for work in mid/advanced career positions.

ENTRY LEVEL/NEW TO THE FIELD	MID/ADVANCED CAREER POSITIONS
Knowledge: –The connections between objects and ideas –The institution's mission, audiences, operations –Cultural sensitivity –Disciplinary content (the museum's area of specialty) –Other methodological approaches that can illuminate the museum's area of specialty: (open ended list): archaeology, bibliography, anthropology, historiography, material culture, education, folklore, sociology, psychology, natural science, etc. Skills: –Critical thinking: conceptualization, synthesis, communication	Knowledge: –Resources in other museums or the field of research (collections, exhibitions, resource people) and/or the field of research –A graduate degree Skills: –Organization –Technology use (data bases, photography, recording, word processing)–or have access to resources with the needed skills –Exhibition (spatial conceptions, ability to communicate ideas visually) –Ability to "read" objects, connoisseurship –Programming skills (awareness of "interactive" learning, composition, and abilities of intended audiences) –Lifelong learning, continuing education –Mentoring, both as a teacher and student –Collaboration, "team" ability

4. Given the list of knowledge and skills the groups has identified, what type(s) of training offerings will provide adequate coverage?

KNOWLEDGE/ SKILLS	CONTENT CONSIDERATIONS	LOGISTICAL CONCERNS
1. Understanding connections between objects and understanding 2. Methodological content 3. Knowledge of other institutions/the field 4. Cultural sensitivity 5. Critical thinking 6. Audiences	1. From the field, exhibitions, curators, consultants, educators, books, classrooms, 2. University, classroom experience 3. Professional meetings, journals, networking, catalogs, case studies in the classroom, visiting other institutions 4. Can begin in the classroom, greater interaction with people 5. University, classroom experience 6. University, consultants	1. Ongoing visiting to other institutions with peers Annual Meetings-structured exhibit revue, staff field trips, general exhibition review 2. Research time/sabbatical programs, concentrated academic experience or in a museum with peers, ICOM, institutes–long and short–including a need for creative ways to fit the needs of working professionals 3. Professional time/release time 4. Recruitment of staff, management and board

5. In the spirit of being true "consumers," are there any other burning issues on your minds related to professional training? If so, please articulate them, and note why you think they are issues requiring timely consideration.

We need to train people to break through the remaining barriers between the academic and museum fields, so that a more complete and complex picture of scholarship emerges.

We need to train people to do research that can act as a catalyst, enabling museums to be socially responsible institutions and agents of social change.

We need to train people to be aware of the fact that there is a multitude of diverse, complex cultures, and that each is worthy of note.

The members of the Training Consumers: Research and Scholarship working group were—

Deborah Smith, Curator of Paper, The Strong Museum (Discussion Leader)
John Alviti, Director, Atwater Kent Museum
Candace Lee Heald, Director of People and Places Program, Freedom Trail Foundation
Gretchen Sorin, Consultant, Springfield Center, NY
Elizabeth Brick, Student, Cooperstown Graduate Program (Recorder)

Training Consumers: Small Museums

Introduction

The Small Museum working group defined the knowledge and skills required to work effectively in a small museum. We noted first that personnel in small museums require generic skills which cut across traditional areas of responsibility. We agreed also that smallness is not a reason for lesser quality. Small museums have an obligation to manage their collections and institutions professionally and up to generally accepted standards.

As we worked we were struck by the frequency that general managerial and people skills came to the fore, often before museum content issues. We grouped skills and knowledge into two lists. We found that all are basic and few were extraneous, so we prioritized the lists. Priority List One contained those skills which we felt were necessary to survive. List Two includes those necessary to be successful.

The "essential to survive" list has people-related, practical skills. This list is not inclusive but it does cover the high points. The "necessary to be successful" list adds more administrative skills a well as most of the traditional museological skills.

In the area of mid-career training we focused on the honing or improving of management skills–those that will make mid-level personnel better at what they are doing. We felt that content training in an individual's specialty is particularly important. It provides intellectual stimulation and refreshment to remind people why they chose museums for their careers.

We believe that training accessibility will be increasingly important in the future. Accessibility includes topics from location and funding to provision of child care. We see training as coming increasingly from state and regional organizations and from institutions outside the profession, such as colleges and seminars. We foresee more exportable training.

In summation, we see the typical small museum professional as a person grounded in an dedicated to material culture who manages a cultural organization that looks suspiciously–or disturbingly–like a small business.

William Galvani
Discussion Leader

---

1. Articulate the knowledge and skills necessary to do the particular job in history museums suggested by your group's title.

KNOWLEDGE	SKILLS
Administrative knowledge	Public speaking/communication skills with individuals and in meetings
Budget preparation and monitoring	Listening skills with Board and others
Long-range planning	Trustee psychology–know when to pick battles, when to back off
Ethics	Educating the Board
Personnel management/policies	Patience/tolerance/getting along with different community groups, social groups, and personalities
Fundraising/grants	Community participation
Risk management/insurance/liability/tax	Proper chemistry with Board
Building/mechanical systems/maintenance/security	Salesmanship
Dealing with contractors and services	
Public relations	
Collections management/registration/acquisition/storage	

73

KNOWLEDGE (continued)	SKILLS (continued)
Conservation for non-conservators Preservation and restoration Exhibits Interpretation/education Publication/editing/writing Content knowledge/specialty Computer literacy	Leadership in many sectors: Board, staff, friends groups Time management Being a self-starter (initiative, being one's own boss) and a self-stopper (when and how to say no) Using skills of others; using consultants Volunteer management Recordkeeping Effective utilization of skills of staff and volunteers

2. Place the knowledge and skills in priority order according to 1) basic and/or essential, 2) useful but not essential, 3) increasingly more important.

PRIORITY ONE	PRIORITY TWO	INCREASINGLY MORE IMPORTANT
Management/administration Goal setting/resource management Long-range planning Subject knowledge/competence in history	Technical knowledge/skills (basic museum skills; exhibits, collections, interpretation)	Long-range planning Fundraising Legal liability/risk management Time management Networking and collaboration Computer literacy

3. Organize the knowledge and skills as to whether they are necessary for entry into the field or for work in mid/advanced career positions.

ENTRY LEVEL/NEW TO THE FIELD	MID/ADVANCED CAREER POSITIONS
Subject knowledge of field Relationship between the ideal situation and reality Public speaking skills/writing skills Interpersonal communication Museological skills Leadership skills	Marketing, fundraising, and development Writing and communications Management and leadership skills Networking–how to employ and profit from it Time management/effectiveness/productivity Content information for intellectual stimulation

4. Given the list of knowledge and skills the groups has identified, what type(s) of training offerings will provide adequate coverage?

KNOWLEDGE/ SKILL	CONTENT CONSIDERATIONS	LOGISTICAL CONCERNS
Working with the Board	Board manual Mediation skills Communication/presentation skills Listening skills Personality types Group psychology/group dynamics Non-profit motivation Board development/motivation	National or regional meeting and pre-meeting workshops Non-museum speakers
Administration (non-profit)	Accounting Budgeting Sales management Fundraising Endowment/portfolio management Building and grounds maintenance Audience identification	Variety of providers: Local colleges (e.g. accounting classes) State museum organizations/regional organizations Private sector seminars National organization/travelling seminars
Museological skills	Collections care and management Exhibitions Education Volunteer management Research	Variety of providers: State, regional associations
Long-range planning	Goal setting Empowerment Execution of goals	Two modes: General session–one day with trustee One-to-one consultancy/mentoring–as follow-ups

Continuity of training–dependability of availability–know training will be available next year or year after–on a regular basis

Not scheduled competing with major meetings

Scheduled for off-season

Participants have same levels of understanding–selection/screening during pre-registration

Length of training: how long will trainee be away from job, family

Cost as opposed to length of training

Scheduled during work week, not weekends

Where applicable, a continuing format, e.g., monthly for x months, or weekly for x weeks

Should be funded by institution

Long lead time in announcing training courses to enable institutions to budget money and time

Avoid overscheduling to allow time for reflection, museum visits

For small museums, taking to site *via* publications, video tapes, items which can go *to* the site. This could be greatly improved

Consider the needs of handicapped and non-traditional attenders

5.   In the spirit of being true "consumers," are there any other burning issues on your minds related to professional training? If so, please articulate them, and note why you think they are issues requiring timely consideration.

Prototype development. Information clearing house. Prevent re-invention of the wheel

Small museums and proliferation

Small museums and collaboration

Content training which provides intellectual rejuvenation/stimulation. An antidote to intellectual burnout/fatigue

Board investment in staff development. Board must financially support staff training

Mentor guidance/relationships

Individual career training and planning

Making training accessible through notification/ information. State or regional clearing houses for training information

Involvement of minorities in museum profession. Lack of role models for minorities. Difficult for women to enter top management

Accreditation as a training opportunity

How to educate your Board without getting fired; sometimes you can be so right, you're wrong

The members of the Training Consumers: Small Museums working group were—

William Galvani, Director, Nautilus Memorial/Submarine Force Library and Museum (Discussion Leader)
Gerald Bastioni, Director, Kemerer Museum of Decorative Arts
Susan Gangwere, Site Manager, Sunnyside, Historic Hudson Valley
Alvin Gerhardt, Executive Director, Rocky Mount Historical Association
Peter Jemison, Site Manager, Ganondagon State Historic Site
Michael Anne Lynn, Director, Stonewall Jackson House
Hilarie Hicks, Student, Cooperstown Graduate Program (Recorder)

ISSUES DISCUSSION GROUP REPORTS

Institutions vs. Individuals
Museology vs. Subject Content
Real Life and Logistical Concerns
Impact of Cultural Diversity

Institutions vs. Individuals

The title of the workshop Institution *vs* Individuals is perhaps how many individuals perceive their relationship with the institution for which they work. The group participating in the workshop would have preferred the title to be "Institution=Individual." Indeed, if collections are a museum's most important asset, of next importance, and even equal importance to some, are the individuals who collect, preserve, study, exhibit and interpret these collections. Yet, little attention is paid to the needs of museum professionals.

A recent study, *The Museum Labour Force In Canada; Current Status And Emerging Needs*, states that: "The collective evidence clearly shows the need for serious rethinking of our approach to human resource development in the museum labour force—. Museums have small operating budgets in proportion to the size of their capital assets (collections and buildings)—. The question of the appropriate balance of human and capital investments—is a basic issue underlying much of the future planning in this area." The study goes on to indicate that: "In fact, there is clear evidence that low salaries and limited investments in professional development are significant problems for the museum labour force—. The common cause of both salary and training restrictions is limited budgets for human resources." The study is "able to conclude from both the quantitative survey data and the qualitative evidence (from case studies and interviews) that museum employees are only moderately satisfied with the quality of working life within the museum sector."

There was no question in the minds of those who attended the workshop that professional development and training opportunities are necessary and that they impact directly on the individual's ability to perform his or her current job as well as on career advancement. The group, however, was looking for more than career mobility and higher incomes. Indeed, the findings of the Canadian study "tend to dampen the view that training truly ensures career progress. In general, the use of training and the amount of training taken, show no significant relationships with indicators of career progress or mobility." Instead, the group focused on job satisfaction and

personal growth. The key issue became the need for institutions and for training providers to articulate and validate the personal development of the individual as being as important as the professional development of the individual. Discussion centered around the need to recoup, rethink, to look anew at one's self, one's job and one's field.

"Museum employees are only moderately satisfied with the quality of working within the museum sector."

The need for specific training in areas that have practical applications and can impact immediately on the individual and the institution, and the need for credentialing and re-credentialing the mid career professional, are givens. But treating the whole person, not just the professional, is neither acknowledged nor provided for. When it does happen, as it does in some programs or at some conferences, it is an indirect outcome, not a goal. It needs to be faced directly and provided for by both institutions and training providers. Personal goals, life-style choices, and family needs have to be taken into consideration as training programs develop their structures and as museums think through how they organize and utilize staff.

Training providers, for example, need to build into their programs opportunities for mid-career professionals—most of whom by this stage in their careers supervise one or more staff people—to learn how to supervise, how to guide, and how to direct, taking into account the personal needs of the individuals they supervise. They have to learn how to use performance evaluation as a tool to identify the personal as well as the professional needs of employees so that work plans are developed that can truly be achieved. Professionals must be able to understand organizational behavior as a reflection of varying personalities and styles, and must learn how to affect change, taking into account issues that may sometimes have only peripheral relationship to work. Managers must be able to incorporate people into decision making so that everyone feels a part of the process. They must also understand that who you are as a person, and knowledge of who others are as people, is necessary to working together and being productive as professionals.

"In general, the use of training and the amount of training taken show no significant relationships with indicators of career progress or mobility."

In addition, training programs have to take into account the personal constraints on their students and prospective students, offering non-traditional schedules and flexible programs. Equally important are programs that encourage both formal and informal opportunities for students to interact with each other. Students are not just professionals who have come for training. They are people who need to share, socialize, brainstorm and learn from each other. Concomitantly, institutions need to demonstrate a responsibility to the whole individual as both a professional and a person. Time off and time out are often crucial to the mid-career professional who is not only dealing with a demanding job, but also, perhaps, young children, aging parents, a divorce, illness, and/or other personal obligations. Only a few organizations have worked out a system of sabbatical leave, but those professionals who have been able to take advantage of it have found it invaluable.

"Only a few organizations have worked out a system of sabbatical leave, but those professionals who have been able to take advantage of it have found it invaluable."

The director of the Bronx Museum of the Arts is pursuing a graduate degree this year at Harvard. The Director of the Payson Gallery of Art at Westbrook College spent a semester researching the collection in Europe. Just as corporations are

rethinking how staff is utilized and structured, museums, too, will have to work out solutions that take an employee's personal needs into account. It is particularly difficult for small museums, but small corporations are forming consortia to solve issues of insurance, child care, paternity leave and so forth. Small museums ought to do likewise.

Museum accreditation by the American Association of Museums should be determined on the basis of excellence as it pertains to staff

"Institutions need to demonstrate a responsibility to the whole individual as both a professional and a person."

management as well as collections, program, and fiscal management. For this to happen, an important first step must be research. How many museum workers are there? What do museum workers need to stay in the field beyond mid-career? How many trained professionals are we losing? Why are we losing them and where are they going? How do museum professionals determine job satisfaction and what is its relationship to productivity? What models exist in the corporate sector that might be adaptable to museums? Canada, with only 10,000 museum workers, has undertaken such a study, while the United States, with an estimated 50,000 workers in 1981, has not. The 1980 Belmont Conference on Mid-career Museum Training acknowledged that there was a lack of statistics. In 1989, there was no additional information available to the participants in the Cooperstown Conference. If such a study results from this conference and if training providers become advocates for training the whole person, not just the professional, the conference will have been a resounding success.

Linda Sweet
Discussion Leader

Student Recorders
Johanna Metzger
Helen Psarakis

Research and scholarship play a vital role in shaping the institutional character and life of local history organizations. Local history museums, historic houses, sites, and societies are just as much places of ideas as they are places of objects. While size and complexity or organizational structure–collections, facilities, staff, exhibits and program offerings, and operating budget – ultimately determine the range and intensity of intellectual activity at the institutional level, the pursuit of knowledge (artifactual and historical) is a common concern for all local history organizations. In this respect, ideas, developed and nurtured through research and scholarship, are indeed institutional building blocks – agents in organizing and documenting material culture collections, planning and implementing interpretive programs, and identifying and developing audiences and constituencies.

A number of factors, internal and external to the local history community, have encouraged this current pattern of institutional development. First, there has been a considerable increase in academically trained historians who have joined the ranks of museum professionals over the past decade and a half. This trans-professional migration has set in motion an "intellectual diffusion" of the most recent research methodologies and interpretive frameworks from the academy *to* the museum, making the "new" social and cultural history accessible to even the smallest and most remote local history organization. This so-called "trickling-down" of academic-based scholarship has been greatly encouraged by the role of the National Endowment for the Humanities as the "public patron" for many local history projects. By making the participation of "academic humanists" a requisite for funding, the thematic content of interpretive exhibits and programs have become more sophisticated and interesting, as well as more historically accurate. But, more importantly, NEH's encouragement has stimulated the development of professional networks and intellectual alliances between the academy and the local history organization, fostering cooperation and collaboration in research and scholarship about the nation's historical past.

Another factor which has helped shape the intellectual spirit of the local history organization has been the increasing importance of these institutions as educational resources. The corresponding rise in the professional prestige of the

> **"Local history museums, historic houses, sites, and societies are just as much places of ideas as they are places of objects."**

curator of education, the creation of educational collections, and the number of out-reach programs which serve individual schools and whole districts has been significant. It could be argued that the past two decades in the institutional development of the American history museum has been one of an "Era of Education." In this regard, the programmatic function of local history museums has achieved parity with the institutions' long-standing curatorial importance. The planning and implementation of intellectually challenging programs, supported by newly established educational collections and other institutional resources, has significantly improved the *interpretive* power and value of the local history museum. Programming, especially for school age children, has provided curators and educators alike with countless opportunities to expand and refine the thematic focus and intellectual foundation of their respective institutions.

A third area of influence has been the demand for improved public access to our nation's artifactual heritage. This has resulted in a greater

> **"Another factor which has helped shape the intellectual spirit of the local history organization has been the increasing importance of these institutions as educational resources."**

accountability regarding the development and care of material culture collections, encouraging curators and collections managers to better document the artifacts in their charge. This documentation initiative has stimulated a nation-wide movement to establish uniform criteria for organizing information related to the material culture collections in our nation's

---

"The local history organization has come to rival the popularity and importance of the community library as a place to go for specialized knowledge."

---

conserving institutions. The cumulative effect of the effort will provide scholars for all disciplinary fields with new-found opportunities to revisit America's past. In addition, the general public has also been the prime mover for elevating the social value and cultural importance of the local history organization as a community resource. The increase in leisure-time dollars and hours for the average American has made the notion of "life-long learning" a recreational ideal. The programmatic response to this cultural trend–primarily through exhibits and programs–have made at least a portion of the American public a new type of intellectual consumer of American history. As a result, the local history organization–museum, house, site and society–has come to rival the popularity and importance of the community library as a place to go for specialized knowledge. If intellectual inquiry and discourse are the spiritual brick and mortar of local history organizations, then the mission statements of these institutions must provide an explanation of their respective intellectual focus. It is not enough to simply tell the public that a local history museum or society exists "to collect, preserve and interpret" the history of a particular community, historic structure, or historical period. Indeed, local history organizations need to establish intellectual agendas and corresponding strategic plans for accomplishing research and scholarship that is needed to sustain their operations. The discussion about the character and quality of an institution's intellectual life should not be framed in

terms of the conventional debate of *museology* vs. *subject content*. Knowledge, which is of value to the functioning local history organization, is far more integrative and holistic in nature; its reduction to an either-process-or-content proposition seriously limits its usefulness. The discussion of the relative importance of intellectual inquiry with a local history organization must center around the inter-relationship that exists among four core areas of research and scholarship: artifactual, historical, educational, and ideological.

Artifactual knowledge involves scholarship that emerges from the "generic" and "contextual" analysis of objects when organizing and documenting material culture collections. This type of inquiry needs to be recognized and encouraged as a distinct form of scholarship. However, it is imperative that such research and scholarship be linked to other forms of historical evidence, especially the more traditional written record, and to the more interpretive-focused scholarship that leads to exhibits and programs. In improving the intellectual merits of such collections management tasks, museum professionals must seek improvement in three areas: in the technical staff's understanding of American history; in the uniform criteria for organizing and documenting collections around critical historical themes; and in disseminating the information learned about the holdings of specific institutions.

The development of the historical content of exhibits and programs involves a second level of

---

"Among many in the historical community, the historical synthesis offered by the local history organization carries with it a long–time stigma of second class citizenship."

---

intellectual activity. This type of knowledge comes from a body of scholarship that produces an *interpretive synthesis* based on the secondary research of the monographic scholarship of academics and the primary research of material documentation by museum professionals. Historical synthesis is a credible intellectual goal for the local history organization. The visual and interpretive nature of its exhibits and programs makes it possible to interpret complex historical themes and issues–human migration, cultural diffusion, inter-group conflict, community formation–in a concise, yet intellectually responsible fashion.

Despite the interpretive power and value of an exhibit's or program's historical synthesis, the

---

"Research and scholarship about the way the general public learns about the past through interpretitive exhibits and programs are critical to the intellectual life of the local history organization."

---

scholarship upon which it is based has not yet been fully embraced as intellectually legitimate and professionally meritorious. Among many in the historical community, the historical synthesis offered by the local history organization carries with it a long-time stigma of second class citizenship. Understanding and accepting the real merits of this type of intellectual activity must come both from the "academic" and the "public" sides of the professional fence. Academic historians need to develop a greater respect for curators and educators working in the local history organization as serious students of our nation's past. As researchers and scholars, museum professionals look to the academy for intellectual cooperation and collaboration as equal partners in the task of better understanding the meaning of the past; not as some historical junkies looking for a quick "academic fix" for their upcoming exhibit or program. In turn, public historians need to develop a greater self-respect for their

own work. To do this, they must take seriously the need to develop the criteria and mechanism for a more formal critique of their scholarship and a way to disseminate their research in a manner other than the conventional exhibit catalog and program pamphlet.

The centrality of the interpretive exhibit and program as "instructional" modes makes the local history organization a very special type of learning environment. Historical museums, houses, sites, and societies, offer a more informal, flexible, and democratic atmosphere to teach meaningful historical issues and concerns. Their use of various forms of visual and audio media requires a multiplicity of senses in order to understand complex ideas and historical themes. Research and scholarship about the *way* the general public learns about the past through interpretive exhibits and programs are critical to the intellectual life of the local history organization. Evaluation of visitor behavior–cognitive and affective–through the ethnographic study and analysis of exhibit viewing and program participation is necessary. To carry out this level of intellectual activity, local history professionals must rely upon the wisdom and counsel of educational ethnographers, developmental psychologists, audience surveyors, and even market analysts to better understand how they provide their multiple audiences–adults, children, families and inter-generational groups–with different kinds of opportunities to learn about the past.

John Alviti
Discussion Leader

Student Recorders
Hilarie Hicks
Diane Kereliuk

We began this discussion by noting that many of the real life and logistical obstructions to professional training are set up by our own attitudes and mind-sets, and those of the people supervising us. For instance, we limit ourselves by looking for training opportunities only within our own profession (i.e., exhibitor, educator, curator, registrar, etc.) rather than looking at the other professions to see what they offer that could be of value across those professional lines. This, of course, is due in part to the feeling that we must justify to our supervisors *why* we should go to this conference or that meeting. It's always easiest to justify it by noting the number of sessions directly appropriate to one's own profession.

One of the first questions was: "How do you find time for professional development/training if you work for a small organization?" This was countered by the entire group with the opposing question: "How do you *not* find time?" In other words, development is important, and time must be found for training. If we are serious about being professional in the museum field, then we must be able to set aside time for professional development and training.

It seemed necessary at this point to define the difference between "development" and "training," with the group agreeing that professional development should be the overarching phrase meaning the process of bettering one's self, and training (learning how to do your job better) being just one part of the whole picture–with reading, networking with colleagues, and visiting other museums also a part of development. We also acknowledged that there are many different kinds of training ranging from in-house and local training to national meetings.

One of the problems with off-site training is that only a few people get to attend meetings, seminars, and conferences. How and when, if at all or ever, does this training then "trickle down" to the rest of the staff? How can we increase that sharing of experiences? How can people who have been away for training re-enter their every-day worlds and manage to hang on to the excitement and ideas generated at the meeting and at the same time benefit the institution at large?

And how do we train more people per institution, particularly when the institutions in question are small with very limited budgets? Some of the ideas from this discussion were:

"If we are serious about being professional in the museum field, then we must be able to set aside time for professional development and training."

—unstructured collaborative visits to other museums.

—institutional support of professional organization memberships and meeting registrations for entry-level personnel (based on the premise that mid- and upper-level personnel can perhaps better afford to pay their own professional costs).

—utilize local service businesses for "basic training" (i.e., department stores could do some training for security and other "front-line" support people who work with or serve the public in the museum).

—provide a "reading day" for regular staff members so they can spend a certain number of hours each month in self-training.

The need to incorporate support people (security, building engineers, secretaries, volunteers) into the profession was discussed. Suggestions:

–include maintenance staff as a part of the exhibit design team; they provide another point of view as to the viability of the finished design.

—the director should take some time to work with personnel on developing plans for anyone wishing to improve their career potential.

—training can be used as a "perk" for work well done, and as a supplement to salary or wages.

Why do administrators *not* allow entry and mid level staff members to take part in training workshops/seminars?

—fear of being replaced.

—reluctance to train employees who will then take jobs somewhere else (or perhaps become restless with the salary level in a current job).

—lack of understanding of the importance for all museum personnel to take part in formal training.

It was pointed out that often notices of workshops and seminars are mailed too late to be helpful in making plans to allow staff members to attend–and also that the target audience is not always clearly defined. Thus, the training providers must take responsibility for assisting administrators in the process of setting up training for staff members by providing better and more timely promotional materials.

Shifting to the "re-entry" problem, we discussed how an individual can return to the institution after a conference and convey the excitement of having been involved in stimulating discussions and finding new ideas for approaching work at hand. Suggestions included:

—post-meeting presentations to colleagues during work hours.

—support from administration and colleagues to test new ideas (is there envy from other colleagues blocking this?).

—attending a meeting or workshop as a team, with specified goals and crossover outlook— team reports upon return to the institution.

Discussion of salary/wage levels led to the conclusion that the low wages paid in the history museum field cause high turnover rates, which ultimately may cost the institution money. On the other hand, a common practice these days seems to be "salary savings:" simply not replacing a departing person and saving the money already budgeted. This is obviously a short-term financial saving, but it may create more of a problem in the long run.

Student interns may help an institution in need of personnel but without adequate funds for a full staff member. However, students in the discussion group raised the issue of their need to

"We must begin to affect the salary levels of this field."

be paid for their internships. While acknowledging that interns are not necessarily the answer for an understaffed or incapable museum, there can be a mutually beneficial contractual relationship established: the institution has much needed assistance on some well-defined projects; and the intern has an opportunity to find a mentor or role model in preparation for a career in the field.

The roles and responsibilities of volunteers, from docent to board member, in the institution should also be covered in training programs. Changing demographics are also affecting these volunteer roles and needs; this must be addressed in training programs.

Finally, in this discussion we came back to a recurrent theme: We must begin to affect the salary levels of this field. It is unfortunate that museums generally still do not reflect the reality

"Will the field want the professionalism implied in hiring trained students enough to pay the higher starting salaries?"

of current living costs, and yet they require a high level of professionalism from their staff members.

Does the process of raising the salary levels begin with the students? Is it necessary for the students to hold out for better beginning salaries?

Or will they simply lose the opportunity to work in the field by adopting such a stance? Will the field want the professionalism implied in hiring trained students enough to pay the higher starting salaries (thereby raising the salary levels across the board)?

A primary issue which was not addressed at all in this discussion, but which should be considered in any thinking about the real-life and logistical concerns affecting professional training, is that of women in the field.

Despite the fact that women make up a major part of the museum work force, very few of them become major museum directors. Is this because women are not considered for those jobs, or do the women remove themselves from the running even before the selection process begins?

One of the realities is that, no matter how much everyone's consciousness has been raised, the woman still does the majority of the work around the home, even if both spouses hold full-time jobs. Single parenting can be a problem; most single parents are women, so they have the added stress of responding to all of the children's needs. If there are senior parents in need of care, again it is the women who generally give that care. All of these things limit a woman's ability to pursue a career track single-mindedly.

When we have formal training workshops, conferences, or meetings, do we take these things into consideration? Women are more apt to travel with families, so do we provide child care information in meeting materials? Women in certain cultures are perhaps not even allowed to travel, so will they ever be able to participate in training meetings? Should we revise our training programs with this in mind?

Finally, early in the 21st century, "minority" groups will make up the majority in this country. Museums must not only begin addressing these cultural groups in their programming, but they must also make great strides toward changing the makeup of the work force, relative to this greater cultural diversity. However, since Amina Dickerson's discussion group addressed this specifically, I leave it to her to expand on this issue.

In closing, I would have to say that one of the most critical real-life concerns affecting professional training is the concept of professionalism and what it really costs: in liveable salaries and wages; in training programs; and in the change of attitudes toward personnel and volunteers and their traditional roles. The benefits of professionalizing (i.e., development and training) will ultimately far outweigh the costs: increased visibility and communication with the outside community; increased response from funding and revenue sources; increased communication and cooperation within the institution; and a deeper understanding of purpose and mission for the institution.

Kathryn S. Sibley
Discussion Leader

Student Recorders
Tom Ellig
Melanie Solomon

The reporter first acknowledged the role which students played throughout the conference–as both host/facilitator and as colleagues/participants. Because they represent the future of the field, their comments and insights were viewed as particularly meaningful to many in the cultural diversity discussion group. Secondly, the concern, so frequently raised in discussions during the conference, for greater cultural diversity in all aspects of museum work was both surprising and gratifying. It appears that this issue has "come of age" at last and, perhaps, indicates a yet larger trend in the nation. Finally, the report of this discussion group was dedicated to the memory of John Kinard–a pioneer in the African American museums movement, a vocal champion for the representation of people of color in museum exhibitions and professions and a dedicated and eloquent museum professional. With his death in 1989, "a great tree has fallen." The museum field owes him a tremendous debt for his contributions to the field and for the legacy of concern for equity in our institutions which he has left us.

Why multi-culturalism? The initial discussion on cultural diversity focused on the creation of functional definitions for the concept of cultural diversity. Because multi-culturalism is an imprecise term, the various interpretations proposed

---

"What museum must strive for is a policy of openness, for this will help to achieve both balance and inclusiveness."

---

by different cultural groups illustrated the complexity of issues related to cultural diversity. In instituting policies of "equity," "parity" or "inclusiveness," or in seeking to provide access for "multi-cultural," "multi-traditional," or "multi-racial" constituencies, the various connotations of these terms to distinct groups can themselves offend or prove obstructive to true collaboration. In this context, use of the term cultural, which has widely ranging definitions, was deemed almost useless, and there was significant support for the substitution of "tradi-

tion" in its place, especially when documenting and presenting the experiences of African Americans, Hispanics/Latinos, Native Americans, Pacific Islanders and others of color. In seeking common ground on terminology, it was clear that the semantic discourse will, and should, continue. What museums must strive for, however, is a policy of openness, for this will help to achieve both balance and inclusiveness. Even with the best intentions, there are pitfalls. For example, the approach of many institutions in developing separate exhibitions with multi-

---

"The process of creating a truly diverse, culturally sensitive museum begins with a dialogue with the community and cultural representatives intended to create an active, vital process of change within institutions."

---

cultural themes hazards the creation of a false distinction, or suggesting inequitable parallels between what is construed as "mainstream" and "other" cultures outside the norm. Collaboration and dialogue are key to avoid such mishaps.

Perhaps in the process, museums themselves will be redefined, with a focus less on objects and more on people. In addition to definitions, the group considered approaches which would enable institutions to address both cultural differences and commonalities among different groups. At present, few opportunities are available which promote such comparisons. Discussants also felt that while cultural traditions need to be incorporated into thematic exhibitions, there is a valid role for independent institutions informed by the distinct view of a specific cultural heritage. Seeking and creating a balance between these approaches is part of the challenge facing museums. The best results are achieved when there is collaboration across cultural boundaries. When this does not occur, problems arise. For example, Native Americans have many concerns about the "rights" perceived by institutions to "study" them because they are "gone" and thus, cannot speak for themselves. Similarly, consideration of differences must extend to growing class disparity, for such socio-economic distinctions impact perceptions of museums and may discourage attendance by those of different social backgrounds.

How does this agenda move forward? What actions need to be put in motion? Most institutions have no real cognizance of what may be required to be responsive to the multi-cultural agenda. The process of creating a truly diverse, culturally-sensitive museum begins with dialogue with community and cultural representatives intended to create an active, vital process of change within institutions. Truly open dialogue does not make the process less difficult, rather it will identify the sometimes awkward and difficult ways in which the institution must change if it intends to embrace different cultures and traditions. In addition, it will identify people representative of these communities willing to assist the process.

To effect substantial representation in the field will require a serious commitment to fund fellowships, internships, scholarships. Because the sense of isolation is often strong in training programs, enrolling teams or groups of students from various cultural traditions is important to prevent high drop-out rates. (One participant noted, "Why would students even want to come in these institutions?") Mentorships and telephone counseling can also help ease the sense of isolation, providing an anchor and encouragement to entering professionals. Other strategies to create a changed complexion in the field are to provide more exposure to the field and an aggressive recruitment campaign at the secondary school levels–and perhaps even in elementary schools. The science and business communities do an excellent job of this, but careers in museums are not something that young people ordinarily encounter without our initiative. By increasing the visibility of museum professionals in the schools, and in the public, we may help ourselves sow a new generation of museum folks.

Where are the models? For training, John F. Kennedy University's Museum Studies Program has been cited, as have the programs of Bank Street College in New York and the workshop programs offered by the African American Museums Association and the Smithsonian Office of Museum Programs. These are often small, sturdy programs worthy of review and modified replication. But for the most part, we need to challenge the old order, to find new formats and approaches. We need to make things accessible through outreach (literally taking exhibitions, or talks on the road which outline the culturally sensitive exhibition development process for well-regarded efforts such as Field to Factory, to people in the field unable to see the show in its original installation.)

Finally, we must re-examine the scholarship. In developing exhibitions, programs and partnerships it is necessary to ask, "Whose history is it?" In stimulating an environment of multi-traditional efforts in exhibitions, collecting, etc., it is

---

"In developing exhibitions, programs, and partnerships, it is necessary to ask, 'Whose history is it?'"

---

important to realize that the inclusion of multiple perspectives will stimulate a change in the internal culture of the institution and that it will be critical to be responsive to the changes that may be required to create this "new order." This is an opportunity for cross-fertilization, sharing both with staff and public the variety of cultural perspectives on a particular theme, as well as building the basis for true collegial collaborations. Through such heightened communication, it is possible to learn more about how to serve new audiences, about the validity of alternative learning styles and cultural preferences. The significance of other sources, traditional sources, of knowledge and methods of work are added to the culture of the workplace, ultimately replacing a Euro-centric model with one which truly responds to the complexion of our multi-cultural communities.

"Though we eat with separate mouths, we feed one belly."
African proverb

Amina Dickerson
Discussion Leader

Student Recorders
Elizabeth M. Brick
Sherill Hatch

EPILOGUE

Conference Summation: Dennis O'Toole
Follow-up Discussion
Call to Action
Follow-up Activities

My lifelong learning process began a number of years ago at St. Edward's Catholic School in Waterloo, Iowa. My teachers were nuns of the Order of Saint Francis. Sister Mary Clothilda was the school's principal. She was a formidable woman, an enforcer who brooked no violation of the school's many rules of student behavior. The model of logical thought we were taught was that of St. Thomas Aquinas as embodied in the person of Father Paul McDonald, who reinforced instruction by throwing chalk or erasers at the in-attentive. I can tell you that those missiles hurt when they hit.

So, I've asked myself, how would Father Paul wrap up this conference?

I have learned enough since my St. Edward's days that I'm comfortable using a less exhaustive–and exhausting–approach to sum-ming up. My model will be Jonathan Edwards, who, when wanting to compose a sermon, would mount his horse and ride about the woods and fields of his town. When an idea came to mind, he would jot it down on a piece of paper and pin it to his coat. He would return from his ride looking like someone who had been tarred and feathered–and the townspeople knew that his sermon had been composed.

Your thoughts, as expressed during this conference, are my tags of jotted paper. What I make of them are just one attendee's attempt to make sense of our proceedings. I hope each of you will do the same on your own behalf.

So, let's take stock of what has happened. First of all, I hope you all see that already much has been accomplished. Friday's discussions between consumers and providers will be hard to forget. The printed summaries of each interest group's findings, which you now have in hand, are a remarkable resource. A lot of conferences have failed to produce summaries as good as these. For providers, they're like having a ready-made market survey. You have a draft of the OMP survey of current professional development

programs in hand. I hope they will bring that survey to completion. We, in the field, need that information. And copies of the Belmont report are available to give historical perspective to this conference's deliberations.

Where do we stand, then, providing training for history museum professionals? How are we doing?

It seems to me that providers are offering programs that meet the current need for certain sorts of professional training. There are, it seems to me, a sufficiency of entry level programs and of programs for the specialities. There are issues in these areas, however, and they should be ad-dressed: duplication, standards (quality), acces-sibility to minorities, and placement of graduates in jobs. An observation I would make on the cre-dentials issue is: Let's credential the programs and institutions, not license the individuals.

There seems to be a much greater sense of urgency around the matter of mid career devel-opment, the land of burnout and renewal. And no wonder. We have reminded ourselves that museums and the environments they exist in are experiencing changes, perhaps profound changes, as we head into a new century. Can-dace said it all very well. Competition has become intense as museums battle for the leisure dollar. Funders see museums as non-essential (though this is not new). There is a shifting sense of the museum's purpose. There are a variety of ways to describe this shift: from administration to management; from collections to audience; from objects to ideas; from cultural conservator to agent of societal change; from talk of careers to talk of lifestyles; from history of the few to the history of the many. The people in "We, the People," are not one color, but all colors.

Given these changes, no wonder we struggle with the question of what it is we should teach and to whom. Human resources will be the most important resource for museums to nurture in the future. This conference has been an impor-tant step along the road to the 21st century.

On Sunday afternoon we reconvened representatives of the Working Groups and Advisory Committee to summarize and assess conference progress and discuss follow-up activities. We had intended to break the group back into small teams to "brainstorm" the next steps, but the Advisory Committee suggested that a general group discussion would be more appropriate given the tremendous energy output throughout the weekend. Peter O'Connell, an Advisory Committee member, recorded our discussion with great clarity. Mary Alexander led the discussion, and collectively the group articulated the points that follow.

Involve the Field—Define Terms

The conference must not be an end unto itself, the work has just begun, and we must involve the rest of the field in the discussion and next steps. We need to define terms (i.e. mid-career) so that we can move more easily ahead. The museum skills and competencies identified in this conference and their division into training experiences for entry level, mid-career level, and advanced professional staff need now to be critiqued by the larger body of providers and consumers alike. Should there be substantial support for the framework, provider institutions should move aggressively to amend existing training curricula or to develop new ones to address weaknesses in training opportunities.

Convince Museum Leadership

We need to convince our museum leadership of the importance of human resource development. This is a concern shared by our Canadian neighbors. Perhaps one method would be to ask CEO's of organizations that have already implemented cutting edge approaches and policies to take the lead–to prioritize needs, identify providers and seek funding. Patrick Boylan suggested that we find a group of lead institutions to initiate a "Professional Development Charter" (similar to an Equal Employment Opportunity employer) and communicate it in job ads to show institutional commitment to staff development. Also, some training systems need to include commitments by the employers of individuals partici-

pating in the training to implement programs reflecting the training. Trainers should be prepared to provide follow-up support and technical assistance during the implementation stage of follow-up projects. Strong emphasis should be placed on evaluation of the successfulness of the training in bringing about individual and institutional development. We should work through Trustees committees, the Museum Trustees Association and meetings of museum directors to raise awareness of the needs, issues, and opportunities of the conference.

Demonstrate Results—Highlight Models

We should demonstrate how training is connected to results–perhaps through highlighting models of successful ventures. Providers of training need to produce larger "training multiplier effects" through the identification of some standard curricula based on validated prototype programs, the training of trainers, and the development of a national, state and local collaborative network. These collaborations would avoid the "top-down" models so prevalent in the past in favor of two-way communication in which field needs and ideas intersect with the ability of national and regional providers to develop materials and training programs and to disseminate them more broadly.

A national process should be developed to identify and validate prototype programs of general interest to the field and to provide adequate incentives to the sponsoring organization to provide training opportunities for other history museum staff. Such a process is necessary to reduce the waste involved in "re-inventing the wheel" and to move the history field ahead more rapidly. Participants recommended establishing a funding base to disseminate information on successful models.

No Barriers Among Consumer Areas

One example of significant progress was the total lack of defensiveness or "territorial barriers" between the consumer groups at this conference. There was no rivalry between curators and educators, or curators and researchers, or exhibit designers and educators, or administrators and any area. In fact, there was a conscious recognition of the interdependence of all functional areas and a pronounced respect for the necessary contribution of each. Participants agreed that this was a healthy and refreshing move forward and should be communicated to the field.

Funding Agencies' Role—New Initiatives

Of course, the conversation turned to funding, and the group recommended that granting agencies take a leadership role by requesting that organizations indicate the amount of support they provide for staff development. Accreditation and assessment programs were mentioned in this same light. Including staff development and training on questionnaires and applications subtly reinforces the importance of these activities to the field, and especially to museum directors. Private foundations also have a strong role to play in establishing funding programs to encourage historical organizations to make commitments to staff development. It was noted that art museums are trying to establish an endowment to provide training for themselves, and history museums might follow suit. Both the recently developed IMS Professional Services Program and the new NEH category called "Seminars, Symposia and Other Projects" (administered by the Humanities Projects in Museums and Historical Organizations, Division of General Programs) were mentioned. Participants noted that both training providers and funding agencies must address the lack of training opportunities in historical content for mid-career and advanced professionals.

Cultural Diversity a Priority Issue

It was exciting to hear throughout the entire conference that broadening the cultural diversity of our staffs, training, programming, and governance was a priority issue. This concern was articulated in every working group report and in all issue and summary discussions. Participants recognized the efforts of conference coordinators to invite representatives of many museum constituencies to attend and contribute to the weekend's discussion but articulated that historical organizations must find the ways and means to recruit people from diverse cultures into the

historical museum field and to train them in museums skills. This initiative will require a long term commitment to aggressive recruitment, financial support, and the development of programming reflecting the multicultural experience. Amina Dickerson mentioned, as a good model, the NEA-supported Open Dialogues Meetings which are drawing colleagues who are concerned about access and multi-cultural issues. These meetings have influenced a variety of structures and produced independent conferences and numerous sessions at other meetings. The current annual meetings of the Western Museums Conference on "Cultural Leadership, Risks and Rewards," were recognized for moving this agenda forward. Also mentioned was a 1990 conference on minority programming at the New York Historical Society (sponsored by the New York State Council for the Humanities) and a collaborative effort in the planning stages on minority recruitment between the New York State Council on the Arts and the Regional Conference of Historical Agencies.

Broader Geographic Invlovement

Geographic diversity was raised as another concern. While it was recognized that the conference coordinators consciously sought representation from throughout the United States the numbers from the West were nevertheless small and we should be mindful of this situation in any planned follow-up activities. It was suggested that we consider state-by-state representation to ensure balance and geographic equity.

Greater Employee Participation—Changing Demographics

We as individuals feel that it is often difficult to influence our organizations; we need to find a way to put "power"issues aside and help our leaders redefine priorities to include more support for human resources. We noted that museum hierarchies can shut down creative thinking and we need to help institutions move toward greater participation in planning and decision-making, as well as pay more attention to staff development. Employers and trainers alike must acknowledge the changing personal factors affecting the ability of adults to particpate in staff development experiences. These factors include a larger number of individuals who have family commitments which limit their availability to participate in intensive programs located at substantial distances from their homes.

Involve Students—Include Volunteers

Students in attendance were recognized as "active consumers" and the group noted that they should have been more involved in the conference discussions. They should be more active partners in any future dialogue. Also, any new comprehensive training delivery system must include the professional staff, paid and unpaid, of small historical organizations.

More Content Training and Evaluation Skills

Although substantial progress has been made in connecting professional historians in historical museums and societies with those in colleges and universities to provide effective training programs, additional work must be done. Perhaps as importantly, research-oriented professionals and public programming-oriented professionals in history museums and historical organizations must continue to engage in open and respectful examination of their basic assumptions about teaching and learning in light of their organizational missions, priorities, and audiences. The staff of historical organizations must become increasingly competent in skills of program evaluation and visitor research to better understand how to provide their many audiences with appropriate substantive opportunities to learn about the past.

Explore Structures to Keep Discussion Going

We should explore mechanisms or structures that will help to produce more activity than

followed the Belmont Conference from ten years ago. Are some of those structures already in place? Is there a way to work within existing committees of AAM or AASLH? How do we utilize annual meetings? Should the discussion leaders of the provider/consumer teams from this conference continue to meet? Should we pick up on the suggestion from the Belmont Conference and establish a consortium of training providers?

Recommendation for Follow-up Activites

The group then turned its attention to articulating a set of goals that could frame follow-up activities and future agendas. The group made a number of specific recommendations for follow-up activities including recruitment efforts to reach culturally diverse audiences; minority internships; focusing on leadership rather than management training; exploring models for sabbatical programs; and follow-up sessions at annual meetings and conferences during the next year. Participants charged the conference coordinators with the task of drafting a final set of goals based on the group discussion. Mary Alexander reminded the group that each person needs to share the responsibility of disseminating the results of the conference.

I closed the afternoon by issuing a verbal "Call to Action" on three levels: individuals, institutions, and professional organizations and prom-

Candace T. Matelic

Session Recorder
Peter O'Connell

Call to Action

In an effort to represent the collective energy and enthusiasm of the participants at the Cooperstown Conference on Professional Training, and move forward the agenda of advancing human resource development in history museums, working groups and advisory committee members agreed on the following goals:

1. To address human development issues as a top priority for history museums, historical organizations, and their professional associations by 1995.

2. To empower the history museum profession to become more representative of our diverse society through equity in staffing, training, collecting, programming, and marketing.

3. To acknowledge and encourage successful efforts to address human development and equity issues within historical museums, historical organizations, and their professional organizations.

4. To advance the study and development of philosophical and educational premises for history museum practice.

Conference coordinators and participants encourage and support ideas, strategies, actions, policy changes, and special projects that further these goals. We view the conference and these *Proceedings* as a step in what we envision as a field-wide movement. It is our hope that the information generated by this gathering of colleagues will inspire, motivate, and provoke much more dialogue and substantive action. Please join us in this important endeavor. The opportunity is clearly upon us.

For more information on follow-up activities contact:

*AASLH Common Agenda for History
    Museums
MBB–66
National Museum of American History
Smithsonian Institution
Washington, D.C. 20560
(202) 357-4573 or (202) 786-2285*

For copies of these Proceedings *contact:*

*American Association for State and
    Local History
172 Second Avenue North, Suite 202
Nashville, Tennessee 37201
(615) 255-2971*

A wide variety of follow-up activities and recent initiatives have come to our attention since the conference. We mention these as examples of the impact of this type of gathering, with the hope that we will see a "domino effect" of additional efforts to keep the momentum and energy alive. The responses have been organized into categories. We invite you to participate in the dialogue about training needs, issues, and opportunities by completing the Reader Response Questionnaires at the end of these *Proceedings*.

Activities of Professional Organizations

American Association for State and Local History (AASLH)

Education Committee Questionnaire: Even before the conference was over, this follow-up activity began as participants piloted the survey instrument. This questionnaire focused on seminars and workshops, and asked about desired content, format, logistics, and needs (such as childcare, inexpensive housing/travel). It was distributed to AASLH members in the January 1990 issue of *History News Dispatch*. They have tabulated the 600+ responses and the results are being analyzed by the Education Committee. This AASLH committee continues to focus on professional development and training. For more information, contact Jim Vaughan, San Diego Historical Society, P.O. Box 81825, San Diego, CA 92138, or (614) 232-6203.

Long Range Planning Committee: The AASLH Council is currently serving in this capacity and has held three meetings since December, 1988, to redefine the organization's mission; examine the potential markets, services and delivery systems; and clarify the roles of Council, committees and staff. At the most recent meeting (November 1989), the group endorsed a future direction focused on service to its traditional markets through an integrated program of training and publications. The Council will use the conference *Proceedings* to help define curric-ula, formats, and potential partners for collaborative ventures.

Common Agenda for History Museums: Under the leadership of a new steering committee headed by Doug Evelyn (NMAH), and endorsed as a core program of AASLH, the Common Agenda continues its work in the area of professional training. It will use the conference *Proceedings* to help work with the Council in defining curricula for training programs and publications, share information about successful models of professional training, and facilitate the piloting of collaborative training ventures. The Common Agenda continues to advocate more scholarship in history museum collecting and interpretation, and stronger linkages between scholars in the academy and museums.

Session at the 1990 Annual Meeting: In Washington, D.C., September 5-8, 1990. There is scheduled a panel presentation summarizing the conference and discussing its impact on the field. Presenters include: John Alviti, Susan Crawford, Candace Matelic, and Susan Tillett.

American Association of Museums (AAM)

The Committee on Museum Professional Training (COMPT): This new standing committee is committed to following up on the conference by incorporating the conference summary goals into its long range plan, and facilitating an ongoing dialogue between training providers representing academic and mid-career programs, as well as colleagues representing consumers of training. Bryant Tolles, current chair of COMPT, proposed that a small task force be appointed to commence work on a strategy for implementation, developing specific objectives under each of the conference goals to determine priority order, time schedule, people, other necessary resources, end products, measures for evaluation, and provisions for future periodic up-dating. The long range plan of COMPT already calls for defining standards for mid-career training opportunities and continuing to work on a recognition program for all levels and types of professional training.

Small Museums Administrators Committee (SMAC) Marketplace of Ideas: At the 1990 AAM meeting (Chicago, May), the focus of this committee's Marketplace of Ideas was on mid-career training, a direct follow up to the conference. These colleagues addressed what kinds of training they needed, both in content and format, and how they could afford training, both in time and money. Training providers were invited to discuss their continuing education programs.

Conference Follow-Up Gathering of Working Group and Advisory Committee Members: at the 1990 AAM meeting (Chicago), a group met to report on follow-up activities. They discussed strategies for future action and ways to keep the momentum of the conference going.

(AAM is planning to hold a Human Resources Symposia in follow up to the Cooperstown Conference sometime late in 1990 or early 1991. See the section on Cultural Diversity for a more detailed description.)

Office of Museum Programs (OMP)

Survey of Training Opportunities for Museum Professionals: The Office of Museum Programs, the museum studies office of the Smithsonian Institution, provides training to help equip museums in the United States and abroad to better serve their publics. The study and teaching of issues in museum history, theory, and practice define its work. In an on-going effort to hone its mission and focus its contributions to museum training nationally, OMP is working to articulate those elements of a national mid-career curriculum in museum studies that it might most appropriately offer. Toward that end, OMP has commited to working on the *Survey of Training Opportunities for Museum Professionals*. This survey is an important first step toward disseminating information about training opportunities. Those interested in contributing descriptions of their training programs for the survey should contact Teresa LaMaster, Deputy Director, Office of Museum Programs, Arts and Industries Building, Room 2235, Smithsonian Institution, Washington, D.C. 20560.

Training Congress: Teresa LaMaster reported that in response to the need for training in issues of cultural diversity, the Office of Museum Programs developed its first Training Congress for museum professionals entitled "Building Partnerships: Museums and Their Communities." Held in June, 1990, this workshop explored practical issues ranging from board education to exhibition development, with the context of museums' increasing commitment to broader public service. Project oriented workshops were led by a multicultural faculty of national stature. Plenary sessions the first and last days of the Congress placed these practical workshops in a theoretical context.

United Kingdom Museums Association (UKMA)

The *Museum Journal* publishes a quarterly guide to courses, training opportunities and conferences.

Also, as Patrick Boylan discussed in his keynote address, the UK Museums Association has been working on defining the essential requirements for validation and accreditation of graduate and post-graduate basic professional training programs. The Association's final conclusions on these vital issues should be published and available in the near future. For more information contact Patrick Boylan at Leicestershire Museum, 96 New Walk, Leicester, England LE1 6TD.

International Council of Museums (ICOM)

ICOM Committee on the Training of Personnel (ICTOP) Conference: The focus of this conference is "Museum Training as Career-Long Learning in a Changing World," and "Career Development: A Shared Responsibility." Hosted by the Smithsonian Institution, August 5-10, 1990, the agenda includes a report on the Cooperstown Conference. This gathering of international colleagues includes papers on three themes: ethics, training needs, and resources. Based on meeting presentations and discussions, ICTOP will formulate and issue recommendations on international museum training as career-long learning and career development based on a changing museum world. For more information, contact Jane Glaser, 1990 Meeting, ICTOP, Arts and Industries Building, Room 2235, Smithsonian Institution, Washington, D.C. 20560.

Canadian Museums Association (CMA)

Human Resources Development Strategy: Following the completion of the Labour Force Study in February, 1989, the Canadian Museums Association is developing a strategic plan for human resource development within the museum sector. The objectives of the strategies are:

To increase the awareness and involvement of the museum community in addressing human development issues.

To increase the level of investment in human resource needs in the museum sector.

To strengthen employment opportunities in large and small museums across Canada.

To redress labour market inequities in the museum sector that have developed along regional, size of institution and gender lines.

To improve the quality of working life in the museum sector.

To strengthen the skills and knowledge of workers necessary to improve the effectiveness of the work force.

The CMA is responding to a federal policy that will have a fundamental impact on all Canadian museums. Canadian colleagues anticipate that new relationships and support roles will develop between the museum community and restructured National Museums.

Keynote Presentation at the 1990 Trainers Conference: Candace T. Matelic presented an overview of activities and issues in the United States related to professional training, and a summary of the Cooperstown Conference, as a keynote presentation for this third national gathering of Canadian trainers (Montreal, March 29-30, 1990). These conferences are government supported, and the focus of the rest of the meeting was to revise the National Museum Studies Curriculum. Jean Trudel, CMA President (and a participant at the Cooperstown Conference) proposed that one of the next trainers conferences be a joint meeting with American colleagues. Proceedings will be forthcoming. For more information, contact Dianna Thompson at CMA, 280 Metcalfe, Suite 400, Ottawa, Ontario, Canada K2P 1RF.

Regional Conference of Historical Agencies (RCHA)

Board Response to the Conference: The Regional Conference of Historical Agencies serves museums in a 23-county region of central New York State. (It is one of four regional service agencies in the state.) President of the Board, Katie Boardman, reported that the conference was discussed at the December 1989 board meeting. Jackie Day, RCHA Director, and three board members had attended and found the experience stimulating both in formal sessions and informal encounters and that it served to reinforce many of the current and new programming efforts that had been considered "risk-taking." They were also challenged by the discussions, particularly in the area of cultural diversity, and plan to respond in their nominations for new board members and through committee activities.

Association for Living Historical Farms and Agricultural Museums (ALHFAM)

Sessions at the 1990 Annual Meeting: At the 20th Anniversary Meeting of the Association for Living Historical Farms and Agricultural Museums, (Brown University, Old Sturbridge Village and Plimoth Plantation, June 17-21, 1990) there was a session to follow up on the conference and discuss ALHFAM's role as a training provider, particularly for the staffs of 2010. Topics of discussion included the specific consumer needs of ALHFAM members, strategies and plans for future training offerings, potential collaborative training programs and the general concern for supporting human resources. A summary of the discusion will appear in the conference *Annual*.

Changes In Personnel and Policies Relating to Professional Development and Cultural Diversity

Chicago Historical Society: Amina Dickerson and Susan Tillett reported on the conference to department heads during the following week. There was great interest, and several people requested more information on the "megatrends" which emerged. Susan reported that, at the time of the conference, they were considering a request by an Assistant and Associate Curator (both recent mothers) to implement job-sharing or professional part-time work. The very strong focus on management of human resources helped them decide to break with tradition and give professional part-time positions a try. One person accepted the opportunity, one person resigned to accept a part-time professional position closer to home and where day care was an option. The staff saw the policy change as a big step forward.

The senior management staff had a full day retreat in early February to discuss ways for the institution to advance the multicultural agenda. Exhibitions, minority internships, targeting new audiences and improving the visitors' experience by the addition of more welcoming interpreters were all discussed. While it is clear they felt they have a long way to go, a frank and straightforward discussion of staff attitudes and public perceptions was extremely helpful.

The Strong Museum: Marie Hewett reported on the following steps taken since the November conference, both in response to the Call to Action and the Strong Museum's new long-term plan. On the professional development issue, the Strong Museum board has recently approved research leave and a tuition assistance plan for staff members, and a workshop on the role of educators on exhibition teams was planned for the Mid-Atlantic Association of Museums Con-

ference (March 29, 1990). On the issue of cultural diversity, the Strong Museum prepared an application for an internship program for minorities to the New York State Council on the Arts, and an African American has recently joined the education staff.

Historic Hudson Valley: Susan Gangwere reported that since the conference several managers began management training seminars arranged for them by the institution's Human Resources Director. These one-day seminars were offered in the Westchester area by a professional business training group, Fred Pryor Seminars. The site managers attended sessions on time management and supervisory skills. This action reflects top management's recognition of continuing education needs among the managers in the hope that we will manage our own staffs and our work loads in a better way.

National Museum of American History, Smithsonian: Doug Evelyn reported that since the conference, they have taken several actions in the areas of staff training , recruitment, and the increased mobility of culturally diverse staff. The principal effort in the first category has been a survey of existing training and analysis of the best approaches to provide needed additional training to large groups of employees. Planning and budgeting for training is complicated by their large size and has been decentralized and largely left to individual offices. In 1989, NMAH provided outside training to 75 employees, over 20% of the staff, and inside training in computer applications, cataloging, and collections management to approximately 150 others. (There is some overlap, of course.) Now they are taking a more coordinated approach. They have recently established a training committee and written policy, as well as a central fund to supplement unit funds.

Aggressive efforts by the Museum since the early 1980's to increase the cultural diversity of its staff and programs have resulted in several curatorial appointments, including one department chair. Recruitment is underway as well for the new program in Hispanic American culture, and NMAH plans to expand programming in Asian American culture as well. The Native American program is well established and regularly involves Native American interns and fellows.

Aside from recruitment to staff for these focused programs, they have recently improved the recruiting procedures to widen the pool of applicants for all positions. Supervisors will be responsible for working with the administrative office to identify organizations, mailing lists, and other vehicles for reaching skilled minority applicants for all of our jobs. Recruitment announcement procedures will be tailored to the needs of the specific job and the applicant pool for that position. They have also taken steps to broaden the pools by developing internships, attending job fairs, and making other presentations about opportunities at NMAH. To advise and support these efforts, NMAH has established a cultural diversity committee drawn from minority staff in the museum. The director has given highly visible leadership in regard to broader programming, recruiting, and staff development, and supervisors are rated in part according to their effectiveness in these areas.

Colonial Williamsburg: Denny O'Toole reported that CW is actively addressing minority access to the profession in some significant ways. The development office is currently seeking funding for minority fellowships for attendance at the Seminar in Historic Administration, and Peggy Howells is working with the other co-sponsors and the African American Museums Association in trying to reach prospective minority applicants. In December, 1989, CW announced the strongest policies it has yet embraced in the area of equal opportunity employment and advancement. Henceforth, no director or manager level position may be filled without a good faith effort to find qualified minority candidates being first made by the hirer. Limited funding for minority internships was approved and the Human Resources Division has intensified its efforts to find qualified minority candidates and to build interest among college and high school students in pursuing careers in museums. Finally, each major division at CW has been required to set minority and female hiring targets for 1990 and to establish strategies for achieving those targets. They are using data about minority and female employment patterns in the Standard Metropolitan Statistical Area to

identify those job categories and work units where these groups are underrepresented at CW.

The Valentine Museum: Karen Holt Luetjen reported on their recently established minority internship program, created in 1986 in recognition of the small number of minority staff members in museums across the nation. In 1987, Phillip Morris USA awarded funds to sponsor three years of the program. Applications are reviewed by staff, who select students on the basis of both their expertise and interests. As with any internship, the project is tailor-made for both the student and the museum, and the student is carefully paired with a direct supervisor. Because interns work full time at the museum for a period between 4 and 12 weeks, students obtain new skills in research, curatorial matters, public programs, and museum administration. Interns act as full time staff during their tenure, attending weekly staff seminars, complying with established policies and procedures, and getting involved in museum-wide projects. The museum actively recruits for the internship with an annual fall mailing to colleges and universities, and appearances at career days and recruitment events. Museum staff also discuss the program with university faculty and career planning and placement officers. By offering the first direct museum experience to minority students, the Valentine Museum encourages students to build their resumes and be more competitive in their future search for museum employment.

Recent Initiatives and Programming to Address Multi-culturalism

AAM: Meg McCarthy reported on AAM's recent initiatives which address cultural diversity, noting that AAM has supported these advances in a number of ways–through the Museum Assessment Program for developing institutions, *Museum News,* and through the forum on Native American policy, just to name a few. Along the same lines, AAM developed a track within the 1990 annual meeting to address concerns of museums with collections representing the cultural heritage of minorities in this country. (AAM's annual meeting attracts approximately 3,000 museum professionals each year and offers well over 100 different sessions on a variety of topics to attend. Two to three percent of attendees currently come from black or Hispanic museums, and 6 to 8 of the sessions each year are designed to deal specifically with issues confronting these museums.)

In May, 1990, just before the Chicago annual meeting, AAM gathered together leaders from African American and Hispanic museums to discuss mutual concerns. The primary theme of the two-day program revolved around the subject of collections in its broadest sense. Collections were chosen as a focus because they are at the core of the museums' mission, and the acquisition and care of these collections pose problems for all museums in addition to raising specific and difficult issues for African American and Hispanic museums. The nature of the experience of African American and Hispanic people demands different approaches to collecting, and, in fact, demands expanded definitions of what constitutes a collection. As the museum community at large learns about collecting in African American and Hispanic museums, all professionals will be challenged to formulate a new understanding of museums' responsibility for collecting and to the community. In this way, the topic of collections provided common ground for interesting , insightful dialogue.

Western Museums Conference (WMC):
Kate Sibley reported that the Western Museums Conference made a decision with the 1989 meeting that it would focus its programming during the 1990's on "cultural leadership," addressing such topics as cultural diversity, environmental concerns, ethics, questions of internal management styles, museums and their communities, and social responsibility in general. The 1989 meeting, titled "Cultural Leadership: Risks and Rewards," took on these issues with such session topics as "Empowering Underrepresented Communities," "Preparing for Controversy in a Changing World: The Board's Role," "Creativity, Censorship and Culture," and "Defining Human Values and Meanings in Contemporary Life: The Role of Science and Natural History Museums." In addition to presenting provocative and diverse

topics, the WMC changed its session format, eliminating panel presentations and actively engaging the audience in all session discussions. Response to both the issues and the format indicated that the conferees enjoyed the empowerment of direct involvement. The formation of a "multi-cultural caucus" during the meeting was proof positive that we all have a long way to go before we can feel any complacency about issues relating to cultural diversity and communication.

The subject of the 1990 WMC Annual Meeting is "Crossing Borders, Building Bridges: Defining the Museum's Role in a Changing Community," and we will once again tackle the thorny questions relating to social responsibility and taking a leadership role, both inside our museums and in our communities. The meeting format will be much the same as last year's, with dialogues taking the place of panel presentations for the most part. Discussions will once again address issues of interest to every professional in every kind of museum. This meeting is held in San Jose, California, a city with a reputation for a strong multi-cultural profile. The 1989 bibliography, printed in the Fall 1989, issue of the WMC *Newsletter*, is being updated for this year's meeting, with the addendum to be printed in the Fall 1990, issue of the WMC *Newsletter*. Information about the 1990 meeting may be obtained from the WMC office, 5801 Wilshire Boulevard, Los Angeles, CA 90036, or (213) 857-6307.

Virginia Association of Museums / Museum Education Roundtable (VAM/MER): Workshop for Culturally Diverse Audiences: A collaborative program, "Museums Through Different Eyes," was organized by the Virginia Association of Museums and the Museum Education Roundtable and three institutions in Old Town Alexandria (The Lyceum, Gadsby's Tavern, and the Alexandria Black History Resource Center). It was held on March 5, 1990, and included sessions on defining cultural diversity, researching audiences to develop culturally sensitive programs and exhibits, examples of Brazilian and African American programming and a historical perspective on multi-culturalism. For more information, contact MER at PO Box 506, Beltsville, MD 20705, or VAM, 301-A North Sheppard, Richmond, VA 23221, or (804) 367-1079.

Historic Hudson Valley: Susan Gangwere reported on recent programming earmarked to work with African American and Hispanic audiences. Ever since the late 1970's they have been involved in programming related to African Americans, holding an annual Pinkster festival which highlights the Afro-Dutch Spring celebration. February 1990 programs (including sessions on Africa and the Renaissance, The Shaping of Black New York, and an afternoon with Ruby Dee and Ossie Davis) were a resounding success and very well attended by the local African American community, with standing room only crowds! Many people had not attended the sites before and were eager to learn more about their programs, and some were interested in volunteer opportunities. In an effort to build a bridge to the large Hispanic community in North Tarrytown (traditionally a non-museum going audience in this area), they held an *Encuento*. This was a gathering of Hispanic community leaders at one of their properties which allowed them to make acquaintances and hear perceptions and ideas about the sites, and discuss program ideas for the future. It was well attended, and now they are beginning to explore ways to follow- up the meeting with positive action. Recently, through grant funding, Historic Hudson Valley has produced a Spanish brochure for Philipsburg.

Susan also reported that it was important to have staff support as they continued their program revision. For example, Radiah Sumler, their Interpretive Programs Director, keeps a sharp eye on culturally diverse programming. Radiah was originally hired to develop outreach programs for minority audiences, so she is strongly committed to exploring ways to attract culturally diverse audiences and highlight culturally diverse programs.

Training Initiative for Native Americans: Peter Jemison reported that since the conference there have been numerous discussions among colleagues regarding the professional training needs of Native Americans. As Peter pointed out, African Americans, Asian Americans, Hispanic Americans and Native Americans are not employed by the majority of museums.

Institutions with collections focused on Native Americans are generally staffed by non-Indians. The recent emphasis on cultural diversity has raised the consciousness of some administrators. The creation of the new National Museum of the American Indian will mean jobs, but how will they fill these positions with Native Americans? Peter has raised this question with Robert McCormick, Secretary of the Smithsonian, Carol Huxley, Deputy Commissioner of the New York State Museum, and Candace Matelic, Director of the Cooperstown Graduate Program. There is a consensus that training for Native Americans must begin with renewed commitment and strong interest from all parties to develop continuing education programs and graduate level curricula to assure that when the new museum opens in seven years, there will be a group of trained and credentialed Native Americans to meet the need. The new era of enlightenment must include an acknowledgement of the special concerns of Native Americans for sacred objects and human remains of their ancestors in museum collections–it is an issue of basic human rights.

Colonial Williamsburg: Denny O'Toole reported on the steps that CW is taking to broaden the audience served by their programs and exhibitions. Thanks to Rex Ellis and the excellent staff of African American interpreters and managers he has assembled, CW has developed a strong level of programming in African American history (unrivaled by any museum in the country, they believe) and are committed to making this story a part of every interpretation at CW. Visitors regularly encounter African American interpretation at three exhibition sites: Wetherburn's Tavern and the Benjamin Powell House in town, and the slave quarters complex at Carter's Grove. During the season, they offer a two-hour walking tour of the town called "The Other Half," and a program of African American music and storytelling in the evenings during the summer. CW offers a school outreach program on the subject during the school year, and a variety of living history programs throughout the year at the Hennage Auditorium of the DeWitt Wallace Gallery. Every February, they sponsor a Community History Forum at the Hennage. This provides a chance to present to the townspeople the oral history of their community, with an emphasis on the black community. In May 1990, CW held a special public forum on the black experience in colonial America at Carter's Grove, featuring Alex Haley and Judge Leon Higginbotham.

Funding Initiatives and Sample Programs

National Endowment for the Humanities (NEH)

Humanities Projects in Museums and Historical Organizations Program, Division of General Programs: Marsha Semmel reported that this year the Endowment began supporting two- to-four week seminars for museum professionals on subjects in the humanities. The new grant category is called "Seminars, Symposia, and Other Projects." It replaces the "Improving the Interpretation of Collections" category. Designed to strengthen the abilities of museum professionals to present humanities programs to the public, the category offers support to museums, consortia of museums and universities, and museum professional associations for projects that emphasize humanities content or promote critical dialogue about museum philosophy and practice regarding public programming. The program encourages museums to organize seminars for museum professionals who participate in the interpretation of collections, including proposed faculty and the intended audience. Applicants should call to discuss their proposals. The new category is part of the recently revised guidelines for Humanities Projects in Museums and Historical Organizations. For more information on this exciting new category of funding, contact Marsha Semmel at NEH-General Programs, 1100 Pennsylvania Ave., Room 420, Washington DC, 20560, or (202) 786-0284.

Institute of Museum Services (IMS)

Professional Services Program: Dan Lukash reported that the IMS program provides federal funds through cooperative agreements with professional museum associations. The agreements support proposals to carry out projects designed to strengthen museum services through such activities as technical assistance, dissemination of information, professional development activities, and professional services. Applicants are evaluated by a peer review panel and the applicant must provide at least 50% match for federal funds. For more information contact IMS at 1100 Pennsylvania Ave., Washington, DC 20560, or (202) 786-0536.

Alliance of Historical Service Agencies (AHSA)

Leadership and Management Seminars: Nicky Forsht reported that under a grant from the Institute of Museum Services, the Alliance of Historical Service Agencies, a consortium of the four New York State regional organizations; the Lower Hudson Conference, the Federation of Historical Services, the Regional Conference of Historical Agencies, and the Western New York Association of Historical Agencies, will conduct four seminars during the fall and winter of 1990-91. The seminars are designed to assist directors and other staff charged with major administrative responsibilities in museums and historical organizations with budgets under $200,000. The topics include legal and ethical issues; approaches to personnel issues: board, staff and volunteers; financial management; and marketing and development. The goal of the series is to help the leadership of mid-sized museums and historical organizations, who are unable to attend longer programs like the Museum Management Institute, to better meet the challenges of their work, thereby strengthening their institutions. A secondary goal is to facilitate and encourage networking among the attendees to explore areas of common concern and possible collaboration. The audio and/or video tapes of the seminars and the comprehensive handouts produced will be used by the four service agencies in the future to reach additional audiences.

Virginia Association of Museums (VAM)

Training Program for Senior Museum Mangers: Edie Whiteman reported that VAM is offering a pilot program "Creating an Environment for Museum Growth," in 1990 with the assistance of the University of Virginia's Division of Continuing Education, the American Federation of the Arts and the IMS Professional Services program. The PSP grant will help to support the training program in 1991 as well. The format involves a series of four day-long workshops, to be held in Charlottesville and in Norfolk. The topics are "Strategic Thinking and Managing Stakeholders," and "Stakeholders to Investors: Securing and Managing Support." For more information, contact the VAM at 301-A North Sheppard, Richmond, VA 23221, or (804) 367-1079.

SPECIAL PROJECTS

Thesis on Collaboration and Its Role in Professional Training: Tom Ellig, a continuing education student in the Cooperstown Graduate Program, decided as a result of the conference to do a thesis that would result in a set of guidelines that can be used to explain how museums can use collaborative methods to develop professional training programs. The project will include case studies of collaborative programs in each of the conference consumer areas: administration, collections, education/interpretation, exhibits, research/scholarship, and small museums. Tom will look at four levels of collaboration: within individual museums; museums working with other museums or national agencies; museums working with cultural and academic organizations and museums working with business and industry. The summary will include recommendations and guidelines to develop collaborative training programs in the six areas. The proposed completion date for this project is September 1991. Tom is interested in hearing about possible case studies and would be pleased to hear from any readers. Contact him at the Minnesota Historical Society, 690 Cedar St., St. Paul, MN 55101, or (612) 296-2747.

APPENDICES

Glossary
Conference Schedule
Student Committees: Student/*Proceedings* Review
Participants
Reader Response Questionnaires
    Training Providers
    Training Consumers

Glossary

AASLH: American Association for State and Local History

AAM: American Association of Museums

AHSA: IMS Alliance of Historical Service Agencies

ALI/ABA: American Law Institute/American Bar Association

ALHFAM: Association for Living Historical Farms and Agricultural Museums

CGA: Cooperstown Graduate Association

CGP: Cooperstown Graduate Program

CMA: Canadian Museums Association

COMPT: AAM Committee on Museum Professional Training

FTE: Full Time Equivalent

ICOM: International Council of Museums

ICTOP: ICOM Committee on the Training of Personnel

IMS: Institute of Museum Services

MER: Museum Educators Roundtable

MMI: Museum Management Institute

NAME: National Association of Museum Exhibitions

NEA: National Endowment for the Arts

NEH: National Endowment for the Humanities

NMAH: National Museum of American History

NPS: National Park Service

NYSCA: New York State Council on the Arts

NYSHA: New York State Historical Association

OMP: Office of Museum Programs

RCHA: Regional Council of Historical Agencies

SAA: Society of American Archivists

SPC: Standing Professional Committee

SMAC: Small Museums Administrators Committee

SUCO: State University College at Oneonta

UKMA: United Kingdom Museums Association

VAM: Virginia Association of Museums

VAM/MER: Virginia Association of Museums/Museum Educators Roundtable

WMC: Western Museums Conference

Conference Schedule

Conference on Professional Training
Needs, Issues, and Opportunities for the Future

November 16-19, Cooperstown, New York

Thursday, 11/16/89
1:00 P.M.—5:00 P.M.   Working Group members arrive.

6:30 P.M.—10:00 P.M.   Informal reception and dinner for Working Group members, CGP Headquarters.

Friday, 11/17/89
9:00 A.M.—5:00 P.M.   Pre-conference Working Groups meet to draft documents for conference review and discussion.

1:00 P.M.—8:00 P.M.   Registration, Fenimore House, New York State Historical Association.

7:30 P.M.—8:00 P.M.   Opening Address by Patrick Boylan. Introduction by James Gold, Cooperstown Graduate Association President. Fenimore House Ballroom.

8:00 P.M.—10:00 P.M.   Reception, Cooperstown Graduate Program Headquarters.

Saturday, 11/18/89
8:00 A.M.—8:30 A.M.   Coffee, Fenimore House.

8:30 A.M.—9:30 A.M.   Opening Remarks and Overview by Candace T. Matelic. Fenimore House Ballroom.

9:30 A.M.—10:15 A.M.   General Sessions - Reports from Working Groups by Discussion Leaders. General Session Facilitator: Mary Alexander. Training Providers: National Organizations, Mary Alexander; State and Regional Organizations, Laura Roberts; Structured Programs, Gail Anderson.

10:15 A.M.—10:45 A.M. Coffee Break

10:45 A.M.—12:15 P.M. General Session - Continued reports from Working Groups. Training Consumers: Administration, Salvatore Cilella; Collections, Susan Tillett; Education and Interpretation, Elizabeth Sharpe; Research and Scholarship, Deborah Smith; Small Museums, William Galvani, Exhibits, Barbara Franco.

12:15 P.M.—2:00 P.M.   Lunch. Pick up box lunches at NYSHA Education Building. Time to visit museums.

2:00 P.M.—3:30 P.M.   Issues Discussion Groups meet at various locations at NYSHA and CGP Headquarters. Discussion Leaders: Role of Individuals and Institutions, Linda Sweet; Balance of Subject Content and Museology, John Alviti; Human Needs and Logistical Concerns in the Real World, Kathryn Sibley; Impact of Cultural Diversity on Training, Amina Dickerson.

3:30 P.M.—4:00 P.M.   Break.

4:00 P.M.—5:30 P.M.   General Session/Discussion Group Reports by Discussion Leaders. General Session Facilitator/Wrap-up by Dennis O'Toole, Linda Sweet, John Alviti, Kathryn Sibley, Amina Dickerson.

7:30 P.M.—10:00 P.M.   The Ultimate CGP Potluck, St. Mary's Center, Elm Street.

Sunday, 11/19/89
9:30 A.M.—11:30 P.M. CGA Business Meeting Brunch, CGP Headquarters (CGA members only), or free time to visit local museums.

12:00 P.M.—3:00 P.M. Follow-up discussion for Working Group Members and Advisory Committee, CGP Headquarters.

Conference Committee

Susan Kay Crawford, chair
Elizabeth M. Brick
Eva Nagase

Stacey A. Otte
Mary Edna Sullivan
Joanne Tupy

Registration Committee
Joanne Tupy, coordinator
Jennifer Ackerman
W. Tryone Coleman
Jean Corrie
Eva Nagase
(guest student housing coordinator)

Photography Committee
Catherine Bohls
William Garrison
Jessie Ravage
Debra Swearingin

Food Service Committee
Stacey A. Otte, coordinator
Catherine Bohls
Barbara Ecker
Tamara H. Funk
Deanna Kerrigan
Elizabeth Nosek
Debra Swearingin

Recording Committee
Elizabeth M. Brick, coordinator
Mary Edna Sullivan, coordinator
Thomas Ellig
Sherill Hatch
Hilarie Hicks
Diane Kereluik
Johanna Metzger
George Seeley
Melanie Solomon

Computer Committee
Kenneth Chandler
Jessie Ravage

Driving Committee
Susan Kay Crawford, coordinator
Steven Amato
William Garrison
Suzanne K. Morey
Randall Schon
George Seeley

Proceedings Review Committee

Mary Alexander
Pamela J. Bennett
Douglas E. Evelyn
Peter S. O'Connell
Dennis O'Toole

Michael Smith
Susan Clarke Spater
Bryant F. Tolles, Jr.
Langdon G. Wright

Participants

Jennifer L. Ackerman
Student
Cooperstown Graduate Program

Dr. Edward A. Aiken
Director
Lowe Art Gallery
304 Crouse College
Syracuse University
Syracuse, NY 13244

Martha Aikens
Mather Employee Development
    Center,
National Park Service
P.O. Box 77
Harper's Ferry, WV 25425-0077

Mary Alexander
Program Coordinator, AASLH
    Common Agenda for History
    Museums
National Museum of American
    History
Smithsonian Institution
Washington, DC 20560

Hope Alswang
Director of Museum Aids Program
New York State Council on the
    Arts
915 Broadway, 8th Floor
New York, NY 10010

John Alviti
Director
Atwater Kent Museum
15 S. 7th Street
Philadelphia, PA 19143

Steven F. Amato
Student
Cooperstown Graduate Program

Gail Anderson
Director
Center for Museum Studies
John F. Kennedy University
1500 Sixteenth Street
San Francisco, CA 94103

Luthfi Asiarto
Director of Museums, Jakarta
c/o Asian Cultural Council
280 Madison Avenue
New York, NY 10016

Inez W. Banks
8 Warren Place
Saugerties, NY 12477

Gerald Bastoni
Director
Kemerer Museum of Decorative
    Arts
427 N. New Street
Bethlehem, PA 18018

Eloise Beil
Director of Collections
Shelburne Museum
US Route 7
Shelburne, VT 05482

Richard Bluthardt
Director of Education
Fort Concho
San Angelo, TX 76903

Kathryn Boardman
Associate Curator
The Farmers' Museum
P.O. Box 800
Cooperstown, NY 13326

Catherine Bohls
Student
Cooperstown Graduate Program

Patrick Boylan
President, United Kingdom
    Museums Association
Director of Museums and Arts,
    Leicestershire
96 New Walk
Leicester, ENGLAND LE1 6TD

John Braunlein
Director
Rockwood Museum
610 Shipley Road
Wilmington, DE 19809

Elizabeth M. Brick
Student
Cooperstown Graduate Program

Lonnie Bunch
Curator
National Museum of American
    History
Smithsonian Institution
Washington, DC 20560

Todd A. Burdick
Assistant Director of Interpretation
    and Education
Hancock Shaker Village, Inc.
P.O. Box 898
Pittsfield, MA 01202

Jane Busch
Assistant Professor
Cooperstown Graduate Program
P.O. Box 800, Lake Road
Cooperstown, NY 13326

John W. Carnahan
Consultant
RD 2, Box 231
Wellsboro, PA 16901

Mary Case
Director, Office of the Registrar
Smithsonian Institution
SI Castle Building, Room 114
Washington, DC 20560

Kenneth J. Chandler
Student
Cooperstown Graduate Program

George M. Chappell, Jr.
Student
University of Delaware
97 Amstel Avenue, Apt 19-W
Newark, DE 19711

Richard Chavka
Managing Director
Mount Lebanon Shaker Village
P.O. Box 628
New Lebanon, NY 12125

Salvatore Cilella
Director
Columbia Museum
1112 Bull Street
Columbia, SC 29201

W. Tyrone Coleman
Student
Cooperstown Graduate Program

Ellen Conrad
Training Interpreter
Old Sturbridge Village
1 Sturbridge Village Road
Sturbridge, MA

Valerie J. Coons
Associate Curator of Education
Winterthur Museum and Gardens
Winterthur, DE 19735

Cynthia Corbett
Director
Federation of Historical Services
189 Second Street
Troy, NY 12180

Jean Corrie
Student
Cooperstown Graduate Program

Susan Kay Crawford
Student
Cooperstown Graduate Program

Mariane Curling
Curator
Mark Twain Memorial
351 Farmington Avenue
Hartford, CT 06105

Jean Cutler
Executive Director
Pennsylvania Federation of
    Museums and Historical
    Organizations
P.O. Box 1026
Harrisburg, PA 17108-1026

Rebecca Danvers
Institute of Museum Services
110 Pennsylvania Avenue
Washington, DC 20506

Marguerite d'Aprile-Smith
Senior Editor, Dec Arts
Arts and Architecture Thesaurus
62 Stratton Road
Williamstown, MA 01267

Jacqueline Day
Executive Director
Regional Conference of Historical
    Agencies
1400 North State Street
Syracuse, NY 13208

John H. Demer
Staff Curator
National Park Service
Harpers Ferry Center, WV 25443

Amina Dickerson
Director of Education and Public
    Programs
Chicago Historical Society
Clark and North Avenues
Chicago, IL 60614

Anne Digan
Assistant Curator for Interpretation
Historic Deerfield
P.O. Box 321
Deerfield, MA 01342

Barbara E. Ecker
Student
Cooperstown Graduate Program

Barbara Efrat
Director
Lower Hudson Conference
2199 Saw Mill Road
Elmsford, NY 10523

E. Duane Elbert
Director, Historical Administration
    Program
Eastern Illinois University
Charleston, IL 61920

Thomas R. Ellig
Student
Cooperstown Graduate Program

Rex Ellis
Director
African American Interpretation
    and Presentations
Colonial Williamsburg
Box C
Williamsburg, VA 23817

Douglas Evelyn
Deputy Director
National Museum of American
    History
Smithsonian Institution
Washington, DC 20560

Nichol J. Forsht
Museum Consultant
Mohawk Terrace No. 216
Clifton Park, NY 12065

Barbara Franco
Assistant Director
Museum of Our National Heritage
P.O. Box 519
Lexington, MA 02173

Tomas Ybarra Frausto
Rockefeller Foundation
1133 Avenue of the Americas
New York, NY 10037

Tamara Funk
Student
Cooperstown Graduate Program

William Galvani
Nautilus Memorial/ Submarine
    Force Library & Museum,
Box 571
Groton, CT 06349-5000

Susan Gangwere
Site Manager, Sunnyside
Historic Hudson Valley
150 White Plains Road
Tarrytown, NY 10591

William E. Garland
Professor and Director
Museum Education Program
College of William and Mary
Williamsburg, VA 23185

William C. Garrison
Student
Cooperstown Graduate Program

Alvin Gerhardt
Executive Director
Rocky Mount Historical
    Association
Route 2, Box 70
Piney Flats, TN 37686

Jane R. Glaser
Special Assistant, Office of the
    Assistant Secretary for
    Museums
Smithsonian Institution
A&I Building 2235
Washington, DC 20560

Cheryl M. Gold
Regional Historic Preservation
    Supervisor
New York State Parks, Recreation,
    and Historic Preservation
Saratoga Spa State Park
Saratoga Springs, NY 12866

James P. Gold
Director
New York State Parks, Recreation,
   and Historic Preservation
Peebles Island
Waterford, NY 12188

Larry Goldschmidt
Assistant Director
Stewardship of Historic Properties
National Trust for Historic
   Preservation
1785 Massachusetts Avenue, NW
Washington, DC 20036

Ray Gonyea
Specialist in Native American
   Culture
New York State Museum
Room #3099
Albany, NY 12230

Gloria Gorell
Director of Technical Services
Lower Hudson Conference
2199 Saw Mill River Road
Elmsford, NY 10523

Nancy Groce
Program Officer
New York Council on the
   Humanities
198 Broadway, 10th Floor
New York, NY 10038

Robert A. Guffin
Director
Webb-Dean-Stevens Museum
211 Main Street
Wethersfield, CT 06109

Jan Guldbeck
Registrar
Strong Museum
One Manhattan Square
Rochester, NY 14607

Lynn Harlan
Museum Technician
National Museum of American
   History
Smithsonian Institution
Washington, DC 20560

Sarah E. Haskins
Director
Historic Speedwell
333 Speedwell Avenue
Morristown, NJ 07960

Sherrill E. Hatch
Student
Cooperstown Graduate Program

Candace Lee Heald
Director
People and Places Program
22 River Street
Plymouth, MA 02360

Marie Hewitt
Vice President of Education
Strong Museum
One Manhattan Square
Rochester, NY 14607-3998

Hilarie M. Hicks
Student
Cooperstown Graduate Program

Lisa M. Hisel
Student
University of Delaware
P.O. Box 172
Newark, DE 19715

Field Horne
Box 215
Saratoga Springs, NY 12866

Barbara Howe
Director, Public History Program
History Department
West Virginia University
Morgantown, WV 26506

Peggy McDonald Howells
Administrator of Museum Studies
Colonial Williamsburg
P.O. Box C
Williamsburg, VA 23187

James Huhta
Director
Center for Historic Preservation
Middle Tennessee State University
Box 80
Murfreesboro, TN 37132

Pam Inder
Lecturer, Department of Museum
   Studies
Leicester University
Leicester, ENGLAND LE1 6TD

Peter Jemison
Site Manager
Ganondagon State Historic Site
1488 Victor-Holcomb Road
Victor, NY 14564

Diane L. Kereluik
Student
Cooperstown Graduate Program

Deanna J. Kerrigan
Student
Cooperstown Graduate Program

Deborah Kmetz
Local History Specialist
State Historical Society of
   Wisconsin
816 State Street
Madison, WI 53508

Alice Knierim
Division Head, Museum &
   Educational Programs
Department of Archives and
   History
624 Washington Avenue
Montgomery, AL 36130

Cynthia Kryston
Chief of Interpretation
North Atlantic Regional Office,
   National Park Service
15 State Street
Boston, MA 02109

Liselle LaFrance
Program Director
Federation of Historical Services
189 Second Street
Troy, NY 12180

Peter LaPaglia
Interim Director
American Association for
   State and Local History
172 Second Avenue North,
   Suite 202
Nashville, TN 37201

David R. Leonard
Student
University of Delaware
229 East Park Place
Newark, DE 19711

Cynthia Little
Education Director
Historical Society of Pennsylvania
1300 Locust Street
Philadelphia, PA 19197

Molly Lowell
Associate Director
Mercer Museum
Pine and Ashland Streets
Doylestown, PA 18901

Karen Holt Luetjen
Director of Public Programs
Valentine Museum
1015 East Clay Street
Richmond, VA 23219

Michael Anne Lynn
Director
Stonewall Jackson House
8 East Washington Street
Lexington, VA 24450

Maud Margaret Lyon
Chief Curator of Collections
Detroit Historical Museum
5401 Woodward Avenue
Detroit, MI 48202

Laurie MacCallum
Connecticut Humanities Council
41 Lawn Avenue
Middletown, CT 06457

A. Bruce MacLeish
Curator of Collections
New York State Historical
    Association/Farmers' Museum
P.O. Box 800
Cooperstown, NY 13326

Anne M. Markham
Student
University of Delaware
79 Madison Drive
Newark, DE 19711

Candace T. Matelic
Director
Cooperstown Graduate Program
P.O. Box 800, Lake Road
Cooperstown, NY 13326

James McCabe
Consultant
20 Washington Street
Red Bank, NJ 07701

Meg McCarthy
Director, Meetings and Continuing
    Education
American Association of Museums
1225 Eye Street, NW
Washington, DC 20005

Thomas McKay
Coordinator
Local History Office
State Historic Society of Wisconsin
816 State Street
Madison, WI 53508

Frank McKelvey
Consultant
1926 Rising Sun Lane
Wilmington, DE 19807

Johanna Metzgar
Student
Cooperstown Graduate Program

Rachel Monfredo
Office of Advanced Studies
Winterthur Museum
Winterthur, DE 19735

Suzanne K. Morey
Student
Cooperstown Graduate Program

John Mott
Retired
16 Arnold Road
Fiskdale, MA 01518

Pamela Myers
Head of Exhibitions and Building
    Services
Museum of the City of New York
Fifth Avenue at 103rd Street
New York, NY 10029

Eva Nagase
Student
Cooperstown Graduate Program

Donn C. Neal
Executive Director
Society of American Archivists
600 South Federal, Suite 504
Chicago, IL 60605

Jean Winnie Neff
Director
Tioga County Historical Society
110 Front Street
Owego, NY 13827

Elizabeth J. Nosek
Student
Cooperstown Graduate Program

Peter O'Connell
Director of Education
Old Sturbridge Village
Sturbridge, MA 01566

Carol Brodeen O'Donnell
Director
Monmouth County Historical
    Assocation
70 Court Street
Freehold, NJ 07728

Wilson E. O'Donnell
Executive Director
New Jersey Historical Society
230 Broadway
Newark, NJ 07104

Dennis O'Toole
Vice President of Historic Area
    Programs and Operations
Colonial Williamsburg,
Box C
Williamsburg, VA 23187

John H. Ott
Executive Director
Atlanta Historical Society
3101 Andrews Dr., NW
Atlanta, GA 30305

Lili Reinick Ott
Director
Heritage Row
126 West Paces Ferry Road
Atlanta, GA 30305

Stacey Ann Otte
Student
Cooperstown Graduate Program

Donna Penwell
Museum Director
Colton Hall Museum
City Hall
Monterey, CA 93940

Daniel R. Porter, III
Director
New York State Historical
    Association/Farmers' Museum
P.O. Box 800
Cooperstown, NY 13326

Helen M. Psarakis
Student
Cooperstown Graduate Program

Jessie Ravage
Student
Cooperstown Graduate Program

Debra Reid
Operations Manager
Farmers' Museum
P.O. Box 800
Cooperstown, NY 13326

Bruce Reinholdt
Chief of Education
New York State Historical
    Association/Farmers' Museum
P.O. Box 800, Lake Road
Cooperstown, NY 13326

Stephen Rice
Student
Cooperstown Graduate Program

Laura Roberts
Director, New England Museum
    Association
Boston National Historic Park
Charleston Navy Yard
Boston, MA 02129

Pieter Roos
Curator of Education
Fosterfields Living History Farm
Kahdena Road, Box 1295
Morristown, NJ 07962

Bart Roselli
Assistant Director of Museum
    Programs
Historical Society of Western
    Pennsylvania
4338 Bigelow Blvd.
Pittsburgh, PA 15213

Randall S. Schon
Student
Cooperstown Graduate Program

George B. Seeley
Student
Cooperstown Graduate Program

Marsha L. Semmel
Assistant Director
National Endowment for the
    Humanities
11 Pennsylvania Avenue, Room
    420
Washington, DC 20506

Elizabeth Sharpe
Deputy Assistant Director for
    Public Programs
National Museum of American
    History
Smithsonian Institution
Washington, DC 20560

Kathryn Sibley
Executive Coordinator
Western Museums Conference
5801 Wilshire Blvd
Los Angeles, CA 90036

James Sims
Acting Director
Office of Museum Programs
Smithsonian Institution
Washington, DC 20560

Deborah Smith
Curator of Paper
Strong Museum
One Manhattan Square
Rochester, NY 14607

Melanie J. Solomon
Student
Cooperstown Graduate Program

Gretchen S. Sorin
Consultant
P.O. Box 149
Springfield Center, NY 13468

Neva Specht
Student
University of Delaware
10 Patrick Henry Court
Newark, DE 19711

Jane Spillman
Curator, American Glass
Corning Museum of Glass
Corning, NY 14830

John Stacier
Program Coordinator
Hanford Mills Museum
P.O. Box 99
East Meredith, NY 13757

Ann Crossman Stone
Program Coordinator
Virginia Association of Museums
301-A North Sheppard Street
Richmond, VA 23221

Mary Edna Sullivan
Student
Cooperstown Graduate Program

Jean Svadlenak
Consultant
624 Romany Road
Kansas City, MO 64113

Debra A. Swearingin
Student
Cooperstown Graduate Program

Linda Sweet
Management Consultant for the
    Arts
132 East Putnam Avenue
Coscob, CT 06807

Susan Tillett
Director of Curatorial Affairs
Chicago Historical Society
Clark Street at North Avenue
Chicago, IL 60614

Bryant F. Tolles, Jr.
Director
Museum Studies Program
University of Delaware
301 Old College
Newark, DE 19716

Jean Trudel
President, Canadian Museums
    Association
Museologie, Universite de
    Montreal
33 Cote Ste-Catherine #1601
Montreal, Quebec,
CANADA H2V 2A1

Joanne Tupy
Student
Cooperstown Graduate Program

Wayne E. Wakefield
Museum Technician
National Museum of American
    History
Smithsonian Institution
Washington, DC 20560

Nicholas Westbrook
Director
Fort Ticonderoga Historic Site
Box 390
Ticonderoga, NY 12883

Edith Whiteman
Executive Director
Virginia Association of Museums
301A North Sheppard Road
Richmond, VA 23221

Patricia Williams
Director for Accreditation
American Association of Museums
1225 Eye Street, NW
Washington, DC 20005

Peter A. Wisbey
Curator of Museum Collections
Monmouth County Historical
    Association
70 Court Street
Freehold, NJ 07728

Langdon G. Wright
Associate Professor
Cooperstown Graduate Program
P.O. Box 800, Lake Road
Cooperstown, NY 13326

Peter Zopes
Historical Site Supervisor
Monmouth County Park System
805D Newman Springs Road
Lincroft, NJ 07738

Reader Response Questionnaire: Training Providers

We invite you to participate in the dialogue on training needs, issues, and opportunities by answering the same questions posed to the conference working groups. Please send your response to Candace Matelic, Cooperstown Graduate Program, P.O. Box 800, Cooperstown, New York, 13326.

Please identify your affiliation by checking the appropriate box:

National Organization ☐   State and Regional Organization ☐   Structured Program ☐

1. Using your working knowledge of the field, can you make additional suggestions about the current offerings available for history museums in terms of content, audience, and level? (Please refer to the appropriate working group report.)

2. Assess the strengths and weakness of these offerings. Note redundancies, gaps and any other special characteristics.

3. What attributes and resources does your organization bring to potential collaborative training programs?

4. Are there any restrictions/limitations regarding potential collaboration/partnership efforts that should be noted?

5. Has your organization been a partner in collaborative training programs? Are there specific successful programs inside or outside the field that we should highlight as models?

6. Can you suggest any additional burning issues?

7. Additional comments:

Reader Response Questionnaire: Training Consumers

We invite you to participate in the dialogue on training needs, issues, and opportunities by answering the same questions posed to the conference working groups. Please send your response to Candace Matelic, Cooperstown Graduate Program, P.O. Box 800, Cooperstown, New York, 13326.

Please identify your affiliation by checking the appropriate box:

Administration ☐   Education & Interpretation ☐   Exhibits ☐

Collections ☐   Research & Scholarship ☐   Small Museums ☐

1. Can you suggest additional knowledge and skills necessary to do the particular job in history museums suggested by your title/affiliation. (Please refer to the appropriate working group report.)

2. Place the knowledge and skills in priority order according to : (1) basic and/or essential, (2) useful but not essential, (3) increasingly more important.

3. Organize the knowledge and skills as to whether they are necessary for entry into the field or for work in mid/advanced career positions.

4. What types of training offerings will provide adequate coverage of these knowledge and skills?

5. In the spirit of being a true "consumer," can you suggest any additional burning issues?

6. Additional comments: